PORSCHE
BOXSTER

JOHN LAMM

MBI Publishing Company

First published in 1998 by MBI Publishing Company,
729 Prospect Avenue, PO Box 1, Osceola, WI 54020-0001 USA

The information in this book is true and complete to the best of
our knowledge. All recommendations are made without any
guarantee on the part of the author or Publisher, who also disclaim
any liability incurred in connection with the use of this data or
specific details.

We recognize that some words, model names and designations, for
example, mentioned herein are the property of the trademark
holder. We use them for identification purposes only. This is not an
official publication.

MBI Publishing Company books are also available at discounts in
bulk quantity for industrial or sales-promotional use. For details write
to Special Sales Manager at Motorbooks International Wholesalers &
Distributors, 729 Prospect Avenue, Osceola, WI 54020-0001 USA.

Library of Congress Cataloging-in-Publication Data
Lamm, John.
    Porsche Boxster/John Lamm.
        p. cm.--(ColorTech)
    Includes index.
    ISBN 0-7603-0519-6 (pbk.: alk paper)
1. Boxster automobile. I. Title. II. Series: ColorTech series.
TL215.B586L35   1998
629.222'2--dc21   98-23723

On the front cover: The Boxster production car mixes
tradition and modern design to bring Porsche back to the
top of the automotive game. This shot was taken on a trip
retracing the tire tracks of James Dean on his fatal final
voyage. *John Lamm*

On the frontispiece: The Boxster show car's headlights drew
early praise for the manner in which they updated the
company's traditional one-light feeling but grouped all
necessary illumination in one beautiful industrial design.

On the title page: One of the Boxster's ancestors is the first of
Porsche's purposebuilt race cars, the 550 Spyder, seen here
with a Boxster. This is the type of car James Dean bought to
further his racing career, and it was while driving the 550 to
a race that Dean was killed. *John Lamm*

On the back cover: Top: The Boxster show car, seen here on
the display stand at the 1993 Detroit Auto Show, was the first
public glimpse of Porsche's new car. Unveiled in front of a
packed crowd, the car was an instant hit. Below: Porsche
designer Steve Murkett created this sketch of a roadster
during the early stages of the development of the 986
(Boxster) program. *Porsche AG*

Designed by Rebecca Allen

Printed in Hong Kong through World Print, Ltd.

CONTENTS

ACKNOWLEDGMENTS

Many thanks to Harm Lagaay, who heads Porsche's design department, and the Boxster's lead designer, Grant Larson, who were very helpful both with their Boxster insight and the fascinating design development photos. Rainer Srock, coordinator of the Boxster and 911 programs, and Ulrich Schempp, who led the development team for the Boxster, kindly took time from their busy schedules for long interviews at Weissach. Michael Schimpke and several members of the *Porsche AG* press department in Germany were most helpful filling many requests, while their counterparts at Porsche North America, led by Bob Carlson, were equally helpful. Thanks also to Thos L. Bryant of *Road & Track* and Csaba Csere of *Car and Driver* for their permission to reprint long quotes from their magazines. And to Joe Rusz for his photos of the Boxster production line in Finland.

Porsche designed a hardtop for the Boxster that is made of aluminum and weighs only 55 pounds. Looking like the hardtop on the 550 Spyders raced at LeMans in 1953, the top transforms the car from an open roadster to a quieter close-coupled coupe.

BACK FROM THE BRINK

Looking back now, it seems to make so much sense, though at the time, late in 1991, nothing about Porsche seemed to make sense. Here was the famous German automaker, considered the premier player by so many automobile fans, foundering about. Sales had been sliding since 1987 with no apparent rescue in sight. Those of us on the outside liked to believe Porsche had a recovery plan in the works, but with no proof of it, things looked rather grim. Even Frederick Schwab, president of Porsche North America, admits that after being named to that position in March 1992, "I wasn't positive that we had an independent future."

Now run the tape forward to early 1998. The headline in the business section of the *International Herald Tribune* reads, "Buoyed by Boxster, Porsche Profits Climb." Profits as in $38.7 million in the last six months of 1997, up from $21.3 million the year before. The company estimated it would produce 38,000 vehicles before its fiscal year was out the following June, including Boxsters

being made in Finland because Porsche's German factory was being pressed to its limits.

Shortly after announcing those impressive numbers, Wendelin Wiedeking, Porsche's chairman and the man who orchestrated the company's turnaround, sat down with several automotive journalists to talk about his company:

"We are among the smallest mass car manufacturers in the world, but we are independent. Nobody thought such a small manufacturer would be able to develop a car, to make such investments in the car industry, and then to survive independently. But I think Porsche created a special system, a system that means that we can do our research and development job much leaner, much quicker, and for less money."

He continued, "You have to take into account that the development and tooling cost of the new 911 and the Boxster was 1.5 billion Deutschmarks and compared to the big players this is nothing. They are not able to do half a car for that and certainly not two cars (as Porsche did

Porsche's Boxster represents the first in a new generation of automobiles from the venerable company, models that mark a split from its traditional way of doing business.

with the Boxster and 911). But Porsche has learned to develop its own systems to do this. As long as we are not following the wrong track and trying to be a carbon copy of a big automaker, we are profitable."

There was a time in Porsche's history when it tried to follow a different path, when, Wiedeking points out, "It thought it should follow the tracks of the big auto companies. David should follow Goliath. This was wrong. It is important we are in the David role, not Goliath's. We have to not only follow our own track, but also design that track, build our own road. We have to make sure that we use our size as our potential." As an example, Wiedeking points out how the company's small size allows him to communicate quickly with his worldwide organization.

Porsche unveiled the 928 in early 1977. With a front-mounted, water-cooled V-8 engine, the 2+2 was meant to eventually replace the 911 as emissions and noise regulations made it more difficult to build the rear-engine, air-cooled model. Admired by many drivers, the 928 never displaced the 911 and was discontinued in 1995.

"I think we learned our lessons about handling bad times as well as good times. Now we have prepared ourselves to go into the next century as an independent, and the goal of the whole team is to stay independent. That's the only way to keep the spirit of the company the way we have it today."

Just a half decade ago, Porsche had almost lost it all, the spirit and the independence. In the previous 10–15 years, the automaker had tried to turn away from its production car traditions, from the air-cooled, rear-engine 911 and toward water-cooled, front-engine models. First came a new entry-level model, the 924, which led to the 944 with its turbocharged variations and then to the 968.

To compete in the upper end of the price scale, and to eventually replace the 911, Porsche designed the 928,

To power the 928, Porsche designed this all-aluminum V-8 engine, which featured aluminum cylinder block and heads, two valves per cylinder, 225 horsepower (SAE rating in the United States), and something unique to engines designed by Porsche for its own automobiles: water cooling.

The ultimate form of the front-engine 924/944 chassis was the 968, which debuted in 1991. The car's 3.0-liter four-cylinder engine featured the Porsche-developed VarioCam variable valve timing system used in the Boxster flat-six. The 968 went out of production in 1995.

a 2+2 hatchback with a V-8 and unique styling that debuted in 1977.

All that is over now, as these new models were done away with to make room for the Boxster and the new 911. Were the 924/944/968 and the 928 Porsche failures? Wiedeking states, "I don't think so. These cars were quite successful at some point in time. The 944 was a great success. The key problem, from my point of view today, was that management at that point in time thought the life cycle of the 944 was the same period of time as the 911. But the 944 was competing in another segment, which is different, so they didn't manage the life cycle exactly right.

"The problem with the 928 was that the car was born to stop the 911. And to be born to kill something else was laughed at by the whole world. That's a big point." A believer that Porsche could sell a model slotted above the 911, Wiedeking feels that if the 928 had been created as a second line, not as a replacement for the 911, it might still exist today, then adds, "Of course, it's very simple looking back now."

Looking back now, it's even difficult to remember how dire Porsche's situation seemed in those first years of the 1990s. In just the United States, the company's sales fell precipitously from a high of 30,471 in 1986 to only 3,728 in 1993.

In the middle of all that statistical doom, however, there was hope inside Porsche. Out of public view, new models were being developed. Porsche's design boss, Harm Lagaay, recalls, "In October 1991 we went to the Tokyo Motor Show." That particular auto show featured a number of great show cars, like the Audi Avus. These cars so impressed Lagaay that, "I faxed my studio and said, 'We need to do a show car.' Porsche's board of directors also felt that in those particular circumstances, when everybody was a bit down, it was absolutely necessary for a show car to be done by us personally."

Porsche was in the midst of its very public problems and, "The public may have felt a little bit ambivalent about us," Lagaay points out, but, "On the other hand, we had the 993 (the late 1993 update of the classic 911)

almost going into production. We were focused on that car, saying 'The 993 will make it.' We were absolutely convinced about that car. So we didn't have that much of a depression inside the company."

The situation was sorted out still further early in 1992 when Porsche firmed up its plans for the future. At the end of 1991, plans to build a four-door car, the 989, were scrapped. Lagaay adds that the 989 "was, from a design standpoint, a great success, but just not the right type of car for us. There was even a sister model to it called the 911, but the pair shared few common parts, which would have made them quite expensive."

So early in 1992, Porsche decided that it would design and develop a new duo. The top-line model would be an all-new 911 with the project number 996. A less expensive model, project 986 (now known as the Boxster), would be the other half of the new project offensive. To keep costs contained so the two new cars could be debuted at roughly the price of the cars they replaced (the 993 version of the 911 and the 968), the new pair would be "simultaneously engineered" and thus share development costs. Once finished and in production, the two new Porsches would have numerous common parts, again to save money and keep them affordable.

But while the new 911 would play to an established audience, its "brother," the Boxster, would have to establish itself in a sports car market for which German rivals Mercedes-Benz and BMW were also preparing brand-new models.

On the other hand, while the other two automakers were developing cars they thought the public would like, Porsche was creating an automobile the public had been wanting for years. Lagaay says that in his studio, a car like the Boxster—a two-seat roadster reflecting the company's rich heritage—was every designer's "kitchen table project." It was never a matter of the public considering the Boxster and wondering, "Why would Porsche do that?" but more a question of, "What took them so long?"

Indeed.

CHAPTER ONE

HONORING HISTORY

The worry was that Porsche's history as an independent automaker might be ending. In the early 1990s, it seemed a distinct possibility that very shortly Porsche history would become just a chapter in the big book of another automaker. It had happened or was happening of late to famous makes like Aston Martin, Alfa Romeo, Maserati, Jaguar, and Saab. So why not Porsche?

Those troubled times can't have been easy for many of those inside the company. There was a revolution under way. Some would call it a palace revolt. The company had canceled its new car programs to set the stage for the development of the Boxster (project 986) and new 911 (project 996). Management was looking to Japan as its model for efficient production. Things were in a bit of an uproar, but at least it was the beginning of a new chapter in the company's history, not an ending.

The first chapter in Porsche's story is the history of Ferdinand Porsche. Born in 1875, he studied "electro-technology" as a young man. Porsche's first automotive design was about 100 years ahead of its time. Automakers scrambling to develop electric cars in the late twentieth century to meet upcoming anti-emissions regulations could have looked back to the year 1900. Displayed at that year's Paris Exposition was the Lohner-Porsche, which was powered by electric motors in its front wheel hubs. A few years later, Ferdinand Porsche even built a gasoline/electric hybrid car, and in it he won his class in a race on the day his son "Ferry" was born in 1909.

Hybrid technology—very much in vogue at the end of the twentieth century—is the type of advanced thinking that has long been a part of Porsche's corporate philosophy. In 1906, this attitude so impressed executives at the Austrian Daimler Motor Company that they hired Ferdinand Porsche, then only 31, as their technical director.

Over the next 20 years, Porsche rose to the position of general director at Austrian Daimler, and was awarded the title of "Dr. Ing." Transferring to the Stuttgart arm of Daimler in 1923, he would create many of the Mercedes

Like the Boxster, Porsche's first postwar car was a midengine roadster. Based on many mechanical pieces from the Ferdinand Porsche-designed Volkswagen "Beetle," the 1948 356-001 prototype had the VW's rear engine/suspension package installed backwards in its tube frame to create the midengine layout.

Heart of the first Porsche sports car was the same air-cooled flat-four used in the Volkswagen, but with 1,131 cc and 35–40 horsepower. It was practical considerations such as the need for luggage space that caused Porsche to opt for the VW's rear-engine layout.

Prix cars. As part of this innovative design—and forecasting the Boxster—these famous competition cars had a midengine layout.

Porsche's most significant design, however, was much more sedate and also better known: the Volkswagen we fondly know as the Beetle debuted in 1938 and is still in production in Mexico 60 years later. Among the numerous variations on the Volkswagen theme was a sports car, but like so many other plans, it was put away during World War II.

Porsche's second chapter begins after the war. This also opens the era of Professor Porsche's son, Ferry. (An age that ended in 1998 when Ferry Porsche passed away during the 50th anniversary year of the company's postwar history.) There was much to do. Rebuilding for Porsche began in Gmünd, Austria, where the company had moved in 1944 to avoid the bombing of Stuttgart.

Professor Porsche was being held in prison. To raise cash for his release, Ferry Porsche and his design team signed with Piero Dusio to create a new Grand Prix car for the Italian Cisitalia team. Called the Type 360, it was a remarkable device with a supercharged 1.5-liter flat-12 mounted behind the driver—a la Auto Union and Boxster—and offered the possibility of two- or four-wheel drive. One car was built, but, sadly, limited financing kept the car from ever being raced on the European Grand Prix circuits. It's reported that when Professor Porsche had a chance to examine the Cisitalia, he said he wouldn't have changed a thing on the car.

Plans for the prewar Volkswagen-based sports car were dusted off. This first true Porsche sports car—with the serial number 356-001—had a tube frame and borrowed heavily from the VW. Front suspension, steering, and brakes were taken directly from the diminutive sedan.

Also borrowed were the air-cooled flat-four engine, transmission, and rear suspension, though they were installed backwards as one unit in the Porsche. In the VW, the engine was behind the rear axle. To get better weight balance for the sports car, Porsche's team turned the engine/transmission/suspension around,

cars that made that automaker so famous in those years. He would foreshadow the Porsche firm's interest in turbocharging almost 50 years later when he developed supercharged engines. Credit for the famous Mercedes-Benz Type S, which led to the SS and SSK, is also his.

Not long after Daimler merged with Benz in 1926 to create the firm that still builds Mercedes-Benz today, Professor Porsche left for another automaker Steyr, but then established his own engineering firm in 1931. Located in Zuffenhausen, near Stuttgart, the new company had the name Dr. Ing. h.c. Porsche G.m.b.H.

He would do consulting work for many firms, but Ferdinand Porsche's most amazing technical work in the coming decade was the creation of the Auto Union Grand

creating a midengine layout, as in the Boxster. Although a clever technical solution, this setup had practical problems, like no proper luggage space, so for production the powertrain went back to its VW rear-mounted configuration, which was kept for tens of thousands of production Porsches.

Production of the 356 began in 1948 with the first cars made at Gmünd. A famous colleague of the Porsches, Erwin Komenda, penned the shape of the 356, and those first cars had aluminum bodies. Although more Porsches would be made in Austria, in 1949 Porsche returned to the grounds it still occupies today in Zuffenhausen, Germany. It began making cars there in 1950, and soon all production was centered there.

Almost from the beginning, Porsches were raced, setting endurance records in 1950 and making their initial entry in the rugged 24 Hours of LeMans the following year. First time out, an 1,100-cc aluminum Porsche coupe

Racing and Porsche came to America with the early Gmünd coupes. John von Neumann bought a Porsche coupe and had it converted into this roadster for competition.

Porsche's postwar racing operations began with this aluminum coupe. Entered in the 1951 24 Hours of LeMans, the car finished twentieth overall and won its class, driven by Auguste Veuillet and Edmond Mouche. The automaker's commitment to the classic French endurance race continues today.

finished 20th overall and won its class. This was also the year Porsches were first imported to the United States by the famous Max Hoffman, who put the company in touch with Studebaker. The result of this meeting was a lucrative engineering contract for Porsche that helped fund new facilities at Zuffenhausen. The sad note to 1951 was the death of Dr. Ferdinand Porsche.

Porsche racing quickly followed the cars to America, first with the aluminum-bodied Gmünd cars, then with the America Roadster and the Speedster. In Europe, Walter Glockler put a lightweight aluminum body on a Porsche chassis, raced it as a special, and inspired the factory to create, in 1953, another of the Boxster's predecessors, the 550 Spyder. Entered at LeMans that year, the car

won its class and spurred Porsche into the world of pure-bred sports cars. You could even order a production 550 Spyder, so young actor James Dean did just that.

Porsche 356s were now rolling steadily off the assembly line, number 5,000 finished in 1954, number 10,000 in 1956, and number 25,000 produced just two years later.

The racing department was also busy and in the process created the competition car that inspired the exterior design of the Boxster. During 1957, Porsche began to race the midengine RSK, a beautiful, rounded little roadster that once and for all established Zuffenhausen's race cars as "giant killers." Any doubts Americans might have had about the Porsche's ability to beat more powerful cars were put away at the 12 Hours of Sebring in 1960. An example of the RSK's lookalike successor, the RS60, driven by Olivier Gendebien and Hans Herrmann, beat the likes of Ferrari and Maserati, for the overall victory.

Thirty years later, Grant Larson, a young American working in the design department at Porsche, would photograph RSKs and RS60s at historic auto races in Germany. Filed away in his imagination, those images would be part of the inspiration behind his design of the Boxster show car, which led directly to the production version of Porsche's sports car.

Another American, Dan Gurney, brought Porsche its only Formula 1 victory as an automaker when he won the French Grand Prix in 1962. At the end of the year, Porsche retired from this form of racing as an automaker to concentrate on sports car and Grand Touring events, something it has continued to this day.

First of Porsche's factory race cars was the 550 Spyder. This 550—which is now in the company's museum—was used by the factory to compete in the famous Carrera Panamericana road race in Mexico.

Porsche established its next major landmark in 1963, when the 911 was unveiled at that year's Frankfurt Auto Show. Two years later, the 356 was retired after a production run of 16 years and some 75,000 cars. At the time, Porsche diehards objected to the new model for although it still had an air-cooled, rear-mounted "boxer" engine, that engine was a six. Nonetheless, the new model would stay in production for 34 years. It would lose half its roof to become a Targa model, giving its name to a new body style. The 911 would be offered as a convertible, gain wide fender flares, add turbochargers, and its horsepower would increase by a factor of more than three . . . and it would become another automotive legend.

During the 911's life, Porsche produced some of the most remarkable sports racing cars of the post-World War II era, all of them with a midengine layout like the Boxster. Into the 1960s, Porsche continued to race to win the 2.0-liter class, occasionally turning that effort into an overall victory.

At the end of the decade, however, Porsches began to compete with ever-larger displacement engines. The stubby, aggressive 3.0-liter 908s pointed the way to the higher classes, a course that was set in April 1969, when

Porsche's 914 was its first midengine production car and featured independent suspension, four-wheel disc brakes, and a five-speed transmission. The car's front and rear trunks were smaller than the Boxster's and the detachable hardtop stowed in the rear area. Porsche 914-4s were powered by a VW flat-four, the 914-6s with a Porsche flat-six. *Photo courtesy* Road & Track

Left
A primary inspiration for the exterior design of the Boxster was the shape of the RSK/RS60 race cars from the late 1950s and early 1960s. This RS60 established Porsche's "giant killer" reputation in America when it was driven to an overall victory in the 1960 12 Hours of Sebring by Hans Herrmann and Olivier Gendebien.

Porsche rolled out 25 917s. For the next two years, Porsche soundly beat Ferrari and dominated the world sports car championship. Then Porsche got even more aggressive and created the 917 Can-Am cars, including the 1973 1,100-horsepower 917/30. Other automakers would make forays into the sports racing car world and sometimes win, but over the next two decades a succession of racing Porsches, like the 936, 956, and 962, would dominate the competition.

Naturally Porsche also raced the rear-engine 911, which came in such amazing variations as the early 1970s RSR, their successors, and the 935. *Road & Track* road-tested a 1976 Group 5 935 and got it to 60 miles per hour

Perhaps the most beloved production model from Porsche during the 1950s was the spartan 356 Speedster. Built for the American market and its importer, Max Hoffman, the car's 1.5-liter engine produced 55 or 70 horsepower, and its base price was $2,995, New York.

in just 3.3 seconds, to 100 in 6.1, and through the quarter mile in an amazing 8.9 seconds.

An important figure in this history in the 1960s and 1970s is another member of the Porsche family who proved to be a brilliant engineer. The name Ferdinand Piech—son of Louise Porsche Piech, nephew of Ferry Porsche—began to appear in the days of the 904 and would be woven throughout the history of the company's great race cars, particularly the all-conquering 917s. Ferdinand Piech continues to play a prominent role in the German auto industry. In the 1990s he became known as the man who pulled Volkswagen and its divisions out of the doldrums and back to profitability with line-ups of excellent automobiles.

With the 917, Porsche's transition from the 2.0-liter race classes to the top level of competition was complete. The cars from Zuffenhausen soundly beat the Ferrari 512s from Maranello. This 917 won LeMans in 1970, while Porsche captured the international sports car title in 1970 and 1971.

Other Porsche automobiles came along to supplement the 911. Looking to slide a model in under the 911's price, the company linked up with Volkswagen to produce the 914. Sold as the VW-powered 914/4 (cylinder) or the Porsche-engine 914/6 (cylinder), these cars slot into the Boxster's history as the first mass production midengine Porsches.

Successor to the 914, the 924 began to lose some of the image we expected from Zuffenhausen's automobiles. Introduced for the 1976 model year, the cars proved light and quite nimble, but were front-engine and water-cooled. The next generation version, the 944, was more of a Porsche as it swapped the four-cylinder engine of the 924—just one of its many components bought from the VW-Audi group—for a proper Porsche engine. The 944's powerplant was half the V-8 Porsche had developed for its 928 model. The 944 went even quicker when turbocharging was added to the four, and the cars earned a good reputation on the race track. In 1991, the 944 got a major mechanical and styling update and was redesignated the 968.

The other significant Porsche was the 928, which was meant to eventually replace the 911. Problems ranging from anti-noise and low-emissions rules to ever-tighter packaging were making the rear-engine, air-cooled sports car more and more difficult to keep in line with regulations. So at the Geneva auto show in March 1977, Porsche debuted its sports car for the future. With a water-cooled V-8 mounted in front, the 928 was a larger car than the 911 and aimed at such competition as Jaguar's XJ-S and Mercedes-Benz' 450SL and SLC.

Porsche's 917 development peaked with the series of Can-Am cars designed 917/30. American driver Mark Donohue was instrumental in the development of this 1,000-horsepower race car, and then he drove it to many wins plus an international closed-course speed record.

Like the 924/944/968, the 928 was quite a good car. Also like its smaller colleagues, it wasn't what the world expected from Porsche, the company that had given it decades of marvelous 356s, 911s, and race cars that had their powerplants in back, where Porsche tradition demands it . . . a tradition carried on in the Boxster and its "brother" car, the new 911.

What part does this tradition play in Porsche's approach to its automobiles? Porsche chairman Wendelin Wiedeking points out, "I think tradition is very important for brands. You can't copy tradition. That's the good thing about it, because it's your own and you work a long time to earn it.

"So this is really part of our success story. Other manufacturers have good products, but they have no history. And in a world where the normal customer is maybe not able to understand differences in the technical details between products, the decision process is more or less driven by the brands. And brands are driven by tradition.

"I think the decision process in the future is more based on the brand than on the real product. And anybody who knows sports cars knows Porsche. So we will keep the tradition alive."

Which sounds like a good way to assure future chapters for the Porsche history.

Although it was front-engined and water-cooled, the 944 Porsche was certainly worthy of the company emblem. This 1988 version had a 2.5-liter overhead-cam four with 147 horsepower.

Among the general public, the most desirable of all Porsches are the 911 Turbos. With their wide fender flares, the turbo's intercooler hidden in the rear spoiler, and plenty of horsepower (282 in the case of this 3.3-liter 1988 model), the mighty Turbos were one reason the 928 was never able to supplant the 911.

HAPPY NEW YEAR IN DETROIT

At the 1993 Detroit Auto Show, in the first few days of the new year, European motoring journalists greeted their American counterparts with what were almost the whispers of conspirators:

"You are going to the Porsche press conference, aren't you?"

"Don't miss the unveiling at Porsche's stand, they say it's quite something."

"They'll have them filling the aisles with this one. . . ."

And so it was, with the crowd forcing many of us to watch from the adjoining displays of other automakers. Wendelin Wiedeking, Porsche's chairman; the automaker's chief stylist, Harm Lagaay; and the head of Porsche in North America, Frederick Schwab, pulled the cover off their mysterious show car, the Boxster. Everyone was quite aware this was the model that could shape much of Porsche's future. This must be the car that would part the clouds that shadowed the automaker after several years of ever-more dismal sales. Would it be worthy?

No problem, gauging by the immediate applause and agreeable head-nodding that followed the unveiling. Words like, "Wow," "Wonderful," or "Perfect" were commonly heard. These were not, however, just comments on the car, but expressions of relief that Porsche was back on the right track. Remember, the Boxster's debut took place in a climate in which the very future of Porsche as an independent automaker was doubtful. In the brief seconds it took to reveal the Boxster show car, the question mark over Porsche shrank dramatically.

The answer was a wonderful, rounded little two-seater that reached into Porsche's past and drew elements of shapes that made the automaker so famous in the first place. What we saw echoed in the Boxster was the form that became famous with Porsche RSK and RS60 race cars in the late 1950s and early 1960s. It was even painted silver, the traditional German racing color. This was not, however, just a race car brought forward 30 years, but a new approach to classic lines brought into the 1990s with

Porsche's Boxster show car, seen here on the display stand, was the hit of the 1993 Detroit Auto Show. Journalists and auto executives had crammed the stand for the car's unveiling.

27

Stefan Stark's interior for the show car proved quite popular, viewers liking the mix of silver aluminum and brick-red leather. Although use of the metal would have been impractical in production, the leather's color was retained as an option.

Below
Although Porsche executives were primed to answer all types of questions about the company's future, journalists wanted to just see the still-hidden show car, which looked quite seductive under its draped cover.

such elements as the most up-to-date headlights and taillights . . . and in the front was an intake that hinted at an air-cooled engine.

If you mention the subject of the Boxster and retro design in the same breath to the company's design chief, Harm Lagaay, he points out, "I have a problem with the retro thing. I don't call the Boxster that at all. Things that are taken from the past and unchanged are retro. But if you reinterpret that same thinking, if you really modernize it completely, that isn't retro. Whether in architecture or whatever profession, there are always cycles and days when people look back into history and say, 'How about that, what about this . . . ?' But that doesn't mean it's retro, unless you take it completely as it was."

Lagaay certainly has the credentials to make such a statement. Born in Holland, the designer was first hired at Porsche in 1970, where he stayed for seven years before moving to Ford of Europe to be the design manager of its Advanced Design Studio. BMW was his next stop, beginning in 1985 as the Chief Designer of the BMW Technik studio, where he was responsible for the innovative and highly regarded Z-1.

Back at Porsche in 1989 to head the styling department, Lagaay stayed with the company through its most difficult years and such projects as the Panamericana show car, the stillborn four-door 989, and the very successful 993 updating of the classic 911. Next came the styling of projects 986 (the Boxster) and its sister car, the 996 (the 1998 911).

In addition to being an enthusiastic designer, Lagaay is also an automotive enthusiast. He is familiar not just with the history of Porsche, but of automobiles in general. On his off weekends, it isn't unusual to find him at one of the important vintage car races, driving his Elfin Can-Am car. So Lagaay respects and understands older automobiles, but doesn't care to design a retro car.

Using an obvious race car comparison he states, "If you take a Boxster and put it next to an RSK, I can't see any retro." He points out that if you have a soft, sloping low

Chrysler president Robert Lutz (right) discusses the Boxster's prospects with Porsche chairman Wendelin Wiedeking (center) and the company's design head Harm Lagaay (left). Lutz said to Lagaay, "That's your car, why do you hesitate?" Porsche didn't.

rear end that is not necessarily retro, but it is a return to something that looked good once before and can do so again, ". . . but I don't think you can compare it to an RSK.

"When we said it would be called the Boxster and reflect our days in the 1950s with the RSK, I said do not show those two cars together because you will hurt the RSK." Lagaay's thinking was that next to the show car, which had been carefully developed in the design studio, the race car would look a bit shabby . . . almost too simple because it was a race car and lacks such accepted amenities as door panels. "So I said you shouldn't have those two car exhibited next to each other because you'll hurt history." Since the introduction and success of the Boxster, he adds, "Now I think it's not so touchy anymore. Now you can show them next to each other."

Inside, the show Boxster was trimmed in a brick-red leather, which covered different style seats for the driver and passenger. The former got a more functional seat with such features as leg bolsters to help the driver brace during hard cornering and a pull-up handbrake formed in the right-side bolster. The passenger's seating had a more relaxed configuration with added room and a zippered pocket in the backrest for a custom Boxster jacket also done in brick-red leather. Cockpit storage included bins in the center console and fitted travel cases behind the seats.

Not surprisingly, the other dominant interior color was silver, which was used on metal surfaces around the instrument cluster, on the center console and even on the doors, where metal tubes doubled as door pulls and elements of the side impact safety system.

One charming little feature was a set of four ventilation fans you could see turning. Inspired by Ridley Scott movies like *Blade Runner* and *Aliens*, the slow-turning fans were set behind coarse wire grilles. Lagaay says the fans "... had their lovers and haters, but I think the reason people liked them was it was the first time somebody had looked at a fan and done it in a different way. It tickled their fancy to look at the fan and be able to say, 'Hold on, that means if it's a visible propeller I can actually adjust it myself.' "The idea is, of course, totally impractical. It means the car has to have four fan motors instead of one, and what would happen if a lady with long hair got too close to the fan or, Lagaay suggests, your child one day

says, "Hey, dad, do you know what I did with my sausage this afternoon. . . ?

"I loved the idea," he continues, "but then the associations I get are with zeppelins. We felt that when we had the fans in the show car they must move, but not too fast. So we got an electrical engineer from Weissach and asked if he could make them go slowly. And he did it."

An elegant interior touch was the use of acetate with a tortoise shell look for several of the switches. Perhaps the nicest distinctive item in the interior, however, was the instrument panel. Although the production Boxster has three instruments, traditionally Porsches have had five dials and the designers continued that in the Boxster show car, though now the five were combined in one plain and in glass. Lagaay explains, "I went to Milano to the furniture show and they had some beautiful pieces of glass with light behind them. That's where I got the idea of having the opaque piece of glass and the dials milled-out of the glass from the back, lit from the back and with the pointer as a shadow. It was very difficult." And also as beautiful as it was impractical for production . . . but then, that's what dream cars are about.

At the unveiling Porsche wasn't saying much about the mechanical specifications of this possible production car, though it was obvious it would be midengine and, it was speculated, that it would be a water-cooled four- or six-cylinder powerplant. And the first three letters in the name, "box," made it obvious Porsche wasn't about to abandon the flat "boxer" layout for its engines.

So that was the silver automotive masterpiece that had the crowd so excited at the Porsche stand, a crowd that included many executives from other automakers, men who seemed as anxious as anyone that Porsche's new course be a solid one. Among those looking on was Robert

The hint that Porsche would be making the switch to water cooling for the Boxster were the intakes in the nose of the show car . . . modern inlets in a vintage shape.

Lutz, then the president of Chrysler. A confessed car fan who grew up in Europe, flew jet fighters for the U.S. Marines, and did stints at the upper levels of General Motors, Ford, and BMW, Lutz is not a man to shrink from controversy or hide his opinions. As he scanned the Boxster, Lutz turned and commented to several of us, "If anyone should build this car, it should be Porsche."

Lutz's comment echoed what virtually every automotive journalist and executive was thinking: great car, Porsche is going to be okay.

Building to Show

What Porsche uncovered at Detroit was the result of a fax Harm Lagaay sent from Japan to his studio in October 1991, after a walk through the Tokyo auto show. Begun in early 1992, the Boxster show car was created in parallel with four studies for the proposed production sports car called the 986, the car we now know as the Boxster. Unlike those proposals, which would be under design development for months, the show car design period would last only until August, when construction had to begin.

By the time fabrication was started, the show car already had a name, which, Harm Lagaay explains, "Came in springtime, 1992 when we started brainstorming on names. The board of directors had a very rational approach, they said it was the CSC (Concept Sports Car). I said that sounds too unemotional, too dry."

Credit for the show car's proper name goes to Porsche staff designer Steve Murkett, who wasn't that excited at first about "Boxster." He recalls, "It was one of three or four names I wrote down. You write down likely names and then think 'Okay, just to show I'm crazier than the rest,'

The design period for the Boxster show car could only last from February until August 1992, when construction had to begin in the shops in Porsche's Weissach engineering center.

While the concept car was being made, it became obvious to Porsche's styling chief, Harm Lagaay, that the design direction being taken with his model should be applied to the production 986. The four design themes being worked in another studio were put aside and the show car ideas applied to the production Boxster.

you write down another." That one was Boxster, ". . . and Harm said, 'That's it.' "

Pointing to fellow Porsche designer Grant Larson, Murkett chuckles and says, "He said, 'No,' and I said, 'No,' but Harm said 'Yes.'"

What were the other three or four names? They won't tell us, laughing again and saying, "We may need them yet."

A few days after Murkett suggested "Boxster," Porsche's board of directors was looking at some models for the show car and Lagaay said, " 'I have an idea, I want this name: Boxster.' And they said 'Yes, let's do that.' " Which just proves, Lagaay adds, "You don't need 1,000 people in the marketing department to come up with a good name."

Unlike some automakers, who have their prototypes fabricated by outside firms, Porsche had the Boxster show car made in its own shops at its technical center in Weissach, Germany, home to Lagaay's studios.

"Our people are too proud to have it done anywhere else. They wanted to do it. There was no question. It was done by people who have a love for this sort of thing." And it was something they rarely had a chance to do. Lagaay points out: "The Panamericana was our first show car in many years." Before that, a real Porsche concept show vehicle hadn't been done since one called the "Long Life Car," which was designed to fit "the philosophy in the late 1970s of building a car with such quality that it would endure the life cycles of four other cars by having an engine that would run forever. It was a two-door sedan, but it had nothing to do with sports cars."

Lagaay points out that in those months in which the Boxster show car was being made ready for Detroit, "We didn't really know what it looked like, because it was unpainted, unfinished, and so on."

Nonetheless, they knew enough about the Boxster show car to see a change coming to the shape of the proposed production sports car program. "The 986 was making great progress," Lagaay recalls. "We went through four different design schemes for the 986, and it was in late 1992 that we realized the design theme of the show car was better than all of the other design themes we had been doing. It meant we had to change quite a lot, because the production version didn't look like the show car anymore. So before we even went to Detroit we realized the Boxster show car was the design theme we should have for the 986. When the success was confirmed by the outside world, we knew we had made a good choice."

This acceptance of the Boxster show car shape for the 986, incidentally, also affected the upcoming 996 version of the 911, which has a great deal in common with the 986, particularly the structure and shape of its nose.

So with the decision already made to alter the direction of the production 986 to match the theme of the Boxster show car, Porsche executives made the journey to Detroit in January 1993 to uncover their new baby.

Lagaay recalls, "We had kept it very quiet. Lots of journalists didn't know we would have a show car, and others who heard a rumor didn't think it would be that spectacular. I remember those days quite well. . . ."

The Boxster was shipped out in the last days of December for the early January show. Frederick Schwab, who had taken the reigns of Porsche of North America when the company was headed for its lowest point, recalls the night before the Detroit debut, saying, "We knew we had a surprise, probably the first Porsche surprise ever. We thought we were right.

"We also knew where we thought it had to be priced, which was at the same level as the 968 coupe it replaced. Those were the words we used . . . under $40,000 . . . although nobody believed us because never in the history of our company had we come in on the target."

Porsche's public relations director in the United States, Bob Carlson, recalls: "Porsche had never really done anything like this before. Concept cars were something we just didn't produce. So we didn't really know what to think of the Boxster. I had to write a press release in advance having never seen the Boxster . . . or even a picture of the car. All the press information was in German. We had to have it translated and there were certain things on that car that didn't translate into English. I was constantly on the phone with Harm Lagaay asking what things meant. The switches, for instance, were made of a material that was similar to tortoise shell, but it didn't translate as that."

Fred Schwab injects with a grin, "Harm was talking about the almost romantic feel of the switches and the words just didn't translate."

Carlson continues, "I had to write an all-too-brief press release . . . and it was the first Detroit show I'd ever been to, so I didn't know what to expect. We flew Dr. Wiedeking in and got him right off the plane and into an interview with CNN. It was a delayed broadcast to be shown the following day, so he took the cover off the car, and it was the first time I'd ever seen the Boxster. I thought it was great, but I didn't know what the public reaction would be."

That sense of caution included the show car's name, Carlson recalls: "When we first heard it, we didn't like 'Boxster.' It didn't just roll off the tongue at the time."

"It does now," Fred Schwab continues. "After the show it had so much positive press there was no name other than Boxster that the car could have. The show gave the car its name, no other name was a choice."

The Boxster show car's headlights drew early praise for the manner in which they updated the company's traditional one-light feeling but grouped all necessary illumination in one beautiful industrial design.

We went to Porsche's test track in Weissach to photograph the Boxster. For a mock action shot of the engineless show car, we pushed it down a hill with designer Grant Larson behind the wheel. When the photo appeared in *Road & Track*, it caused a stir among German publications, which didn't realize the show car was only powered by gravity.

Carlson adds, "Now if you sold the car and called it a 986, no one would know what it is."

The press conference loomed ahead. . . .

Like any thoughtful automaker, Porsche does not send its executives into a press conference without coaching them on the company's position on questions that might be asked. Question and answer periods can be deadly for an unprepared company representative, particularly at a time when things aren't going well . . . and haven't for some time. So before the Detroit press conference, Porsche executives who would be in line to answer press questions went over the company's official view on various subjects, both automotive and economic.

It turned out to be unnecessary. The small Porsche stand was off in a corner of the show, which is held in Detroit's vast Cobo Hall. Large, colorful, often noisy displays from the likes of Ford, Chrysler, Mercedes-Benz, Toyota, and all the divisions of General Motors dominate the hall. Diminutive Porsche even had to borrow some chairs to get ready for its press conference crowd, which was expected to be enormous, given both Porsche's difficult financial condition and that tantalizing shape hidden under wraps.

The arrangement of the stand put the company's chief executives in front, facing rows of chairs for journalists, with the as-yet-uncovered show car staged left.

The conference opened with the expected statements from Wiedeking and Schwab, but when the floor was opened for questions, all that preconference preparation proved unnecessary.

There were no questions. Journalists kept glancing to their left, to the soon-to-be uncovered show car. The only question they had was, "What does the car look like?"

So the trio of Wiedeking, Lagaay, and Schwab stepped forward to whip the cover off the new car. Their U.S. public relations manager had already made a point of carefully choosing where to place himself for the grand unveiling. "During the press conference," Bob Carlson explains, "I was standing next to Denise McCluggage (one of America's most respected motoring journalists) who used to race Porsche 550 Spyders. I wanted to be next to her when they took the cover off, and when they did she just said, 'Boy, you've really got it. You really captured the car.' And I thought, 'This might be okay.' "

"We came to Detroit not knowing what to expect," Carlson continues, "and the Boxster ended up being the best of show and on the cover of *Autoweek*. We hadn't had a success like that in a long, long time. I remember Tom Gale (then the head of design for Chrysler) coming out in *Autoweek* and saying what a beautiful design it is."

Schwab also felt that same sense of optimism, recalling, "The reaction of the people attending the show and the press was universal, saying that this car was the sexiest thing around. And with that came the call that we must produce it . . . and we must produce it quickly."

As for the number of non-Porsche automobile executives who were cheering for the Boxster show car at Detroit, Schwab—speaking at the same auto show five years later—says, "We've just came off an excellent year in 1997 having sold 14,000 cars. So in a 15 million-car industry we don't compete with the big automakers. But for people who like and enjoy automobiles we represent the *piece de resistance*. Our car has always been associated with fun, and the more you know cars the more you like our car. So the car people, in the press and in the business, like Porsches. There are Porsche owners everywhere, and I know they want us to succeed."

Harm Lagaay agrees, adding, "Lots of people, who had their own show cars, were coming over to our stand and saying, 'Do it. Do it.' " When Chrysler's Robert Lutz talked with Lagaay he asked, "That's your car, why do you hesitate?"

Porsche didn't, and what we would only learn later is that when the show car was uncovered in January 1993, the 986, the car that would become the production Boxster, had already been through almost a year of development.

From this overhead view, you can see the different seats provided for the driver and passenger. While the driver's seat has more support, the passenger's is meant for comfort. It's a nice idea, but quite impractical for production, which has to allow for such factors as right- and left-hand drive models.

While the response to the Boxster show car was quite encouraging, it alone would have to keep everyone energized for the near future. For after Porsche's success with the Boxster launch at Detroit in January 1993, the year fell apart for its North American subsidiary. "We sold less then 4,000 cars," Schwab points out, "and in our heyday in 1986 we sold over 30,000 cars. None of us, including me,

Among the unique details of the Boxster concept car were these small ventilation fans, which were inspired by the slow-turning fans in movies like *Blade Runner*, and made to turn slowly in the show car. Impractical for production, the fans produced a love-dislike reaction among those who saw the concept vehicle.

believed how bad it could get." This situation didn't ease until the 993 (the new 911) went on sale in April 1994 and Porsche Cars of North America's sales charts finally went on the upswing.

Despite all the glowing press reports about the Boxster launch in Detroit, Porsche didn't allow itself to be blinded by the success of the show car, which made surprisingly few appearances and was then locked away. Several years later, Mercedes-Benz would learn the danger of creating and overusing an exciting, aggressive show vehicle that causes confusion when its production version finally appears. Mercedes' AAVision interpretation of the upcoming M-Class sport utility left many potential customers anticipating one type of vehicle but being sold another.

Porsche didn't fall into that trap. Lagaay explains that the company board "realized it could be dangerous, because you have this pearl, this diamond, but are you going to show it around forever, to the next show and the next show? Obviously we realized that the production Boxster would be different, and you have be careful how you communicate that. We said we are going to communicate it very slowly." So the Boxster concept car was shown at "Geneva in March and Tokyo in the fall and that was it. A lot of people hated me for locking it up, but we were busy getting into the production version."

CONCEPT VERSUS PRODUCTION

The relationship between the Boxster concept car and the final 986 production version is easy to see here. Radiator packaging caused the center front grille to give way to two smaller front intakes. The rear air inlet's size and placement changed, but there's no question the show car's shape led to the final version. One thing that had to be altered was the Boxster's size:

	Boxster show car	Production 986
Wheelbase	94.5 inches	95.2 inches
Track, front	57.9 inches	57.7 inches
rear	58.5 inches	60.2 inches
Length	162.0 inches	171.0 inches
Width	68.5 inches	70.1 inches
Height	48.8 inches	50.8 inches
Tires, front	205/50ZR-17	205/55ZR-16
rear	225/45ZR-17	225/50ZR-16

CHAPTER THREE

THE WEISSACH FACTOR

To any serious Porsche fan, Weissach is paradise. This is the home of Porsche design and development, the place where its famous automobiles are conceived, created, and put to the test. And where, on a warm spring day in 1993, I met with Horst Marchart, who heads research and development for Porsche's executive board.

The Boxster concept car had already made its mark in Detroit, and those of us on the journalism side were trying to find out what would be Porsche's next step with this fascinating new car. Hence our interview for *Road & Track* with Marchart, who was holding his cards necessarily close to his chest.

"We have a classic car in our program, which is the 911," he began. "And we have two other cars, the 928 and 968. Those are good cars, but they are not in the same level as the 911 in image." After telling us the 911 would continue to be part of Porsche's product line, he admitted, "In the future, we will have a two-line program. It is our goal to find a second line, one which comes up to the same level as the 911. And the Boxster is a styling study in this direction."

Marchart quickly made it obvious that the company was not in the process of developing a retro car. "We want to have a traditional feeling in the future . . . but a traditional feeling around modern technology. It was not our goal to find an old car and give it a new shape."

And although this was the era of exotic super cars—including Porsche's own instant-legend, twin-turbo, four-wheel-drive 959—that approach was also not part of Porsche's program. He stated, "We are looking at features for the driver who wants to be happy when he drives the car. It is not the main goal to have the highest maximum speed. That is a secondary goal. The car must be fun. If the driver wants to lower the top, it should be easy to do so. The car should have good ergonomics. A good sound. It should be a sporty car, but it can also be comfortable. It must not be harsh riding . . . that is the direction we will be going."

Perhaps the most brilliant aspect of the Boxster (986) and 911 (996) designs is the manner in which the engineers created two automobiles that share almost 40 percent of the same parts, but are also quite different: the Boxster a midengine two-seater roadster, the 911 a rear-engine 2+2 Grand Touring car. *Porsche AG*

Below and on facing page:
These photographs ilustrate where the Boxster and 911 are most different. The Boxster's 2.5-liter flat-six is tucked in front of the rear wheels, while the 911's 3.3-liter version of the engine sits behind the rear axle.

As it turned out, Porsche had already been working quite hard in that direction for over a year. By late 1991 and early 1992, Marchart and others in a study group had set a model policy for Porsche that would turn away from its then-current multimodel, money-losing course and aim it profitably at the twenty-first century. In a

small book, they established the pair of automobiles Porsche should build, including in it the cars' size, engines, weight, and costs. Also noted was the expected competition, including what was known about sports cars being developed by German competitors Mercedes-Benz and BMW.

One of the most critical elements in that book was the Boxster's price, which had been promised at the Detroit Show as that of the 968 it would replace, which was about $40,000. If there was one fact those at the show and those who interviewed the likes of Marchart and design chief Harm Lagaay in the coming years couldn't

believe, it was that Porsche would meet that price target. Even as late as the day in 1996 when the Boxster price was announced, there were those in the press who were skeptical Porsche could do it. Many assumed the price would creep up to the mid-$40,000s. But Porsche wasn't kidding when it set that price, and I was right to believe Lagaay when he told me in spring 1993, "The main goal is not just to keep the Boxster as good as possible from a design standpoint, but also maintain the price. Price is absolutely crucial. Even as a designer I have to say it's crucial, especially in America."

That goal was just one of many taken on by Ulrich Schempp when he was named Boxster project manager. It was a difficult time at Porsche, given the company's problems in the previous years, but even then he says, "I think the people were very motivated. And they had more fun working on a roadster project than a four-seater (Porsche's then most recent development program), so it was an enthusiastic group."

Schempp recounts, "On February 1, 1992, I got the task to head the half-year study to see if this prescribed car could be realized under those conditions." Before then, "there was nearly nothing, only some studies and the experience," which is no small thing at Porsche. Timing called for the concept studies to be completed by September so vehicle development could begin.

From the start, it was obvious this would not be a new car program as they had been done in the past at Porsche. Schempp explains, "It was clear that not only did we have to make a new car, we also had to make a new project

On these pages
Seeing the head-on view is the best way to note the similarities of the Boxster and 911. Each model has its own unique front valance panel, where the air enters the radiators, but they share the same front fenders, hood, outside rearview mirrors, and doors.

organization. We formed teams for this concept, and later, after the decision was made that the car should be built, we had more teams. I think this kind of project organization was key to the success of this car."

Previously, Porsche would have appointed a project manager for a new automobile, and the development of that model would become the driving force in the program. Only after the chassis had been refined would the production experts be asked to look at the new car to see how it would be built. Later, the sales and service departments would be brought in to give their comments on the new model.

"But with the Boxster these people were involved from the beginning," Schempp explains. "In the design period, the production people were in the design studios and, for instance, they might say this radius can't be done and here we have the possibility to make the tolerances better, and so on. This helped us quickly reduce the development loop so we could save costs and time."

For these same reasons of economy, this new system of simultaneous engineering wasn't being applied to just one model, but two: 986 and 996. The former would become the Boxster, while the latter would be the successor to the famous 911. From the beginning, the pair was developed in parallel programs.

Making things even more difficult was the fact the 986 and 996 were almost totally new automobiles. Usually a development team is called on to design a new body or a new engine, but this group had to do both.

By sharing many common parts, the 986 and 996 would cut costs not only by using the same pieces, but also by saving development time. As a result, the two cars have many like parts, particularly under the skin in their basic "architecture," from the nose rearward to the A-pillar that forms the sides of the windshield frame. This similarity includes their front suspensions. Related parts would also save in production, making it easier to assemble the two cars on the same assembly line. So very quickly it became the development teams' goal to have

One of the prettiest design elements of the Boxster and 911 are their headlamps, which are quite similar, though not identical. To some old Porsche fans, the move away from a single large headlamp with several smaller lights functioning as turn signals and side marker lights was controversial.

similar cars from the nose to the A-pillar and differentiate the 986 from the 996 from there back.

Rainer Srock, who oversaw the development of the two cars, points out, "The aim was that they be developed together, but that they have a difference, which should be as big as possible." Not only would the Boxster be midengine while the 911 would get its traditional rear engine, but even the handling would differ. Srock adds, "There should be a big difference between the concepts, the styling, and the cost so the customer doesn't have to think a long time about which car they prefer."

It was also decided early on that while the two cars would be developed in parallel, the 986 would be finished first and go on the market a year before the 911. It was obvious by the eroding sales of the 968 that Porsche's weakest position was at the bottom end of the market. Before long, the four-cylinder models would be dropped from the showrooms and would need to be replaced first.

Schempp explains, "We had parallel development of both cars, because they were so close together we always had to think, if we do this in this way for the Boxster, how will we do it on the 911? Otherwise, we would have made mistakes, which we could not correct afterwards.

"So for much of the period of development the cars were nearly parallel. Then, maybe 18 months before series introduction of the 986, when all the things were fixed — the engine was clear, the body-in-white was clear — the Boxster went extremely quickly to production, and the 911 was slower, because we had more time."

While pulling the plug on the four-cylinder 968 and V-8 powered 928, Porsche was also putting development time and money into the 993. This model was an update of the venerable 911 design, staged to debut in late 1993 (spring 1994 in America) to bring in badly needed money while the development of the 986 and 996 continued. This revised 911 would prove to be a big hit, though by touting it as the "new 911" Porsche really confused things when the truly new 911 (the 996) finally appeared in autumn 1997. And by making the 993 such a good car, Porsche probably prolonged the argument about how much better the 996 was . . . but that's a discussion for another book.

Also among the investigations that took place beginning in February 1992 were the type of engine and chassis that would be used for the 986 and 996.

When I first talked with Horst Marchart about the Boxster in spring 1993, he hinted that the car would be offered with a four- or six-cylinder engine. As the development of the car continued, however, the four was dropped. Although there were tens of thousands of Porsche 914s, 924s, 944s, and 968s produced with fours, the engine just didn't fit in Porsche's new product image. The Boxster would get a six and it would be flat.

"The main thing from the beginning was to make a flat, boxer engine," Ulrich Schempp explains. "We also had studies with other engines, but a flat engine is typical for Porsche. And for a midengine location a flat engine would be better than a vee engine because it packages better."

It was traditional for Porsche to have a flat engine, as the boxer-four in the Volkswagen Beetle was one of the crucial elements of that landmark design which was inherited by the original Porsche 356.

The engine configuration also helped name the new Porsche. For many years, these flat powerplants with their opposed cylinders have been known as a "boxer" engine because their pistons' outward movements mimic those of a man fighting. So how could a car called the Boxster have anything other than a boxer engine?

Just as obvious from the start is that the new engine would be water-cooled as this solved several technical problems. Porsche engineers had been telling us for many years that it was getting increasingly difficult to meet ever-tightening fuel consumption and low-exhaust emissions regulations with air-cooled engines. This argument was used in the late 1970s to explain the development of the front-engine water-cooled V-8 powered 928. At the same time, it was hinted that for the same reasons the 911 wouldn't be around for many more years, though when owners showed a decided preference for the 911 over the 928, Porsche engineers managed to continually refine the air-cooled flat-six to meet the rules.

Schempp explains, "The problem was that we could not easily make a four-valve engine with an air-cooled engine. There isn't enough room. For a long period, our race cars have had air-cooled cylinders and water-cooled cylinder heads. But if you have the water-cooling system in

Noses of the pair of Porsches are identical, with the same trunk that's so deep it seems to reach right down to the road. Also notice the similar placement of the small, lightweight spare tire and the brake system's master cylinder reservoir.

a production car it would be better also to cool the cylinders with this water and not air. Otherwise you would need a fan to pull this air, and the fan makes noise." Not a good idea at a time when noise emissions rules, particularly in Europe, are becoming more difficult to meet.

Again the 986 and 996 would share fundamentals, their engines based on the same construction principles. Likewise, their cylinders have the same bore centers so the engine blocks can be manufactured on the same machines. From there, the differences begin to show. Each engine has its own specific cylinder heads. Since the Boxster six is a displacement of 2.5 liters and the 911 gets 3.4 liters, they have different bores and strokes. Their intake manifolds are not the same and so on.

Converting to water-cooled engines also presented Porsche engineers with a problem they hadn't faced before: packaging radiators in a sports car with its engine behind the cockpit. Schempp admits, "This was one of the most difficult tasks, fitting the radiators into the car. It was a struggle with Harm Lagaay and his crew and the technicians who are responsible for the radiators to bring this together. We searched in every direction of radiator technology—in the rear, in the front, before the rear wheels, circle radiators—all forms of them to help make a smooth, small car."

Some 14 different solutions were tried. Like placing the radiators behind the cockpit, which proved too wide for good aerodynamics. Finally they settled on three front radiators, two for coolant—as also used in Porsche's famous 959—and one for the air conditioning. Air that flows through these coolers is directed in front of the

On these pages
The "architecture" under the dashboard of both Porsches is almost identical (Boxster at the left, 911 on the right). You can see this in the similarity of their center consoles and the placement of the heating/ventilation/air conditioning controls, the radio, and many of the buttons.

wheels, which has beneficial aerodynamic effects. The air exiting the radiators aids in countering lift in front, and overall drag isn't increased by the air rushing through the radiators. The rear side inlet on the left side is for engine air, while the one on the other side helps lower the engine compartment temperature.

To complete the drivetrain, Porsche would need a pair of transmissions, a manual and an automatic. Schempp says, "We looked for components on the market that we could bring to the cars. In earlier years, Porsche tried more to design and invent every new part for its cars, but it was clear we could not do that this time. It is a strategy at all car manufacturers to bring developed components into the car to save costs and time. Both the automatic and manual transmissions were available, the Tiptronic from ZF, the manual we have together with VW."

In designing the chassis, Porsche gave itself quite a bit of flexibility for the 986, the 996, and the future. Engineers created a front for the pair by establishing how much room they would need to meet all crash and safety standards, space for luggage, a location for the fuel tank, and a front suspension. Once this universal front end was established, the company had the freedom to design a unique rear end for different models, such as the midengine Boxster and rear-engine 911, but with the potential to create still more models that grow rearward from the front end.

MacPherson strut suspensions, with a Porsche design twist, were drawn up for the front and rear of the Boxster. The 996 kept the front suspension of the universal front end, but got its own independent five-link rear design.

Again during the design of the chassis, the fact that the 986 and 996 were undergoing parallel development affected the progress of the program. Schempp explains, "We had to go step-by-step to check up if we had fulfilled the regulations. First we checked if the Boxster was OK and then we checked if the 911, which is a bit heavier, was OK. It was a difficult process."

Above and on facing page
While the pair share much under the skin, their instrument pods are quite different. The Boxster (above) has its dials grouped in three gauges—a la 550 Spyder/RSK/RS60 race cars—with a little hood that lets light through, as on the Boxster show car. Traditionally, 911s have five dials, a layout that was retained for the 996 (right).

It also made a difference that Porsche was developing a pair of automobiles that had their engines in the rear and the fuel tank ahead of the cockpit. So the first line of crash defense is the bumper. Next comes the front structure around the luggage area, which is relatively weak so it can crush in a controlled manner to dissipate and distribute crash energy. Get to the fuel tank and you'll find a very hard structure that protects it.

Another difficult engineering problem was the Boxster's folding top. Schempp points out, "We had a technical engineering goal, a weight goal, and a goal to have a top that could be easily operated." Porsche didn't want it to be like the old 911 top, which folded upon the body and created a tall top "stack" that inhibited vision to the rear. Instead, the Boxster's folding top should completely disappear.

"We tried over a matter of months to do a top that was manually operated," Schempp continues, "but at the time we recognized that this was not easy to handle by some owners. We then decided to make an electric power-operated top. This was rather late in the program, so we had a lot of work to do."

The solution looks so simple and elegant that it belies the engineering work needed to create the folding top system. Unlike most tops, which simply fold and stack, the Boxster's retains the front section intact and allows it to move rearward and down, rather like a letter "Z" folding flat. Schempp explains, "We had to invent a mechanism to manage it." The hidden highlight of this design is the plate inside the top section over the cockpit that forms the upper horizontal of the Z and is made of pressure cast magnesium.

While other automakers might go to an outside firm to have such a complicated and specialized mechanism created, Porsche did the Boxster's top at home in its own engineering group, though it is made by a company jointly owned with Mercedes.

For those who live in areas where the weather can be miserable, Porsche also developed an aluminum hard top that weighs only 55 pounds and has a heated rear window for quick defogging.

Schempp points out that the same thinking that led to the power top affected several systems in the Boxster. "At the beginning we thought the Boxster should be a simple car," he says. "We had no power-operated windows, no power-top operation, and we had no power steering. But during development we recognized that if we want to have women as a big part of our customers, we need power steering. And then we realized we cannot do both power steering and non-power steering models so we decided all the cars would have it."

All this basic work, from those first thoughts right through design and development, was done at such a pace that by February 1, 1994, just two years after the official start of the program, the first prototypes were running. They did not, however, look like Boxsters as we know them.

The first of the three levels of 986 "mules" was based on the modified exteriors of 968 cabriolets. When construction of these early test cars began, the Boxster concept car had yet to score its victory at Detroit and another exterior design was under development for production.

With the show car's success, however, the emphasis shifted to applying that shape to the production 986. The two following levels of prototypes looked much like production Boxsters, but only after a lot of work by the development team.

Schempp points out that at the time of the success of the Boxster at Detroit, "We had done a big step in the development of the production Boxster, and we looked a little critically at this Detroit Boxster. We felt that if this car was chosen it would be an enormous task to change what we had already done. It was, for instance, a little bit shorter. But it was clear the Detroit Boxster looked better than the Boxster we had at the time, so we took on the hard task and I think everybody was delighted to do it because it was a better car."

So the second and third steps up the prototype ladder included cars that were quite close to the final design of the production Boxster. They were painted a matte black in an attempt to hide the exact appearance of the all-new car from what seemed to be the ever-present spy photographers that were dogging the development trail of this important new Porsche.

Primary testing of the Boxster took place at the company's Weissach test facility. This famed engineering center is a half-hour's drive west of Porsche's Zuffenhausen headquarters on a road that is itself a nice little test route. Shortly after leaving the suburb of Stuttgart, the road straightens but then begins to turn and wind about. The countryside is classic for Germany, with small, tightly packed villages set in neatly plowed and very productive farmland. Punctuating the scene are occasional broad

stands of the forests Germans are so proud of, and which they rightfully protect with an almost religious fervor.

As you wind higher out of the village of Weissach, you begin to see the tall trees that hide the test track from the telephoto lenses of those inquiring photographers. Next comes a set of buildings that make up the design and engineering center of the facility. This is where Porsches are designed, clothed with their bodywork, fitted for their functional interiors, built up as prototypes, and then rigorously tested.

This is also where non-Porsches might go through any phase of that same schedule. The automaker is well known as an engineering center that is available for consultation, design, and development for any automaker that cares to buy its services. Most of this work is kept strictly secret, but some is openly discussed. Harley-Davidson and Porsche talk with pride about the German company's development work on the classic American motorcycle engines.

It was in this test track, made legendary as the place where Mark Donohue worked with Porsche in the

In overall views, you can see the basic similarity of the Boxster (above) and 911 interiors. Note how much the seats look alike . . . as they also look like most Porsche seats of the recent past; this means they are both supportive for hard driving, yet comfortable enough for long trips.

development of the amazing 917/30 Can-Am cars, that the Boxsters went through their basic development work.

It will come as a disappointment to many Porsche fans that the one thing engineers *weren't* doing was taking the initial steps to create a Boxster race car. Company chairman Wendelin Wiedeking has made it quite clear that he doesn't want a competition version of the midengine sports car, saying, "Our racing activities will

only be done with the 911. We race with the 911 because it is our top of the line. My intention is that the Boxster and the 911 will not race against each other. It doesn't make any sense to me.

"I have to handle the brand, I have to handle the money, and it doesn't make sense to give money to people who try to beat the 911. This happened in the past in our organization with the 944 Turbo. The project leaders sought to beat the 911. You should beat your competitors, not yourself."

Besides, there was enough work developing the Boxster to keep the engineering staff busy. And it isn't enough just to test in their own backyard, even one as renowned as Weissach.

Porsche took its development team on the road. To analyze the Boxster and its systems—from shocks to engines to heaters—under cold conditions, the mules were taken to America, to Canada and its Northern Territories, and to the frozen town of Arjeplog, Sweden.

By contrast, there also had to be hot weather trials, which were conducted in California's Death Valley. Denver was the place to check the cars for high temperature at high altitude. The car's abilities at even higher altitudes were tested on Colorado's Mt. Evans, which has the highest road in the United States. Durability and more temperature trials were conducted at Nardo, a huge circular track in southern Italy near Brindisi. The French Alps served as a proving ground for the brakes.

Over hundreds of thousands of miles the Boxster engineering prototypes were frozen, overheated, beaten up, torn apart, and generally abused. To watch this happen can be quite appalling to anyone not familiar with the process, particularly as the prototypes get closer to production and look more like "real" cars. But these were the final steps Porsche engineering took in readying the Boxster for manufacture, steps that began back in late 1991 and early 1992 in that little book on which Porsche's future is based.

CHAPTER FOUR

STYLING THE BOXSTER

The exterior design of the Boxster is a natural. And apparently, it was only a matter of time and changing attitudes until a Boxster was created in Porsche's design studios. Harm Lagaay, the man in charge of those rooms and their designers, recalls that when he first went to work at Porsche in 1970, the company's famous race cars—the 550 Spyders and the RSKs—were already represented on the studio's "inspiration boards." These boards are displays of ideas from all over the world—automotive shapes, fashion, architecture, even movies and music—meant to trigger designers' thinking about a new car.

So why didn't Porsche do a Boxster-style of automobile back then? Lagaay explains: "In 1971, the RSKs were only 10 years old, but they were considered to be really old. In those days, cars like the RSK, with a hand-beaten aluminum body, heavy space frame, heavy suspension, and an engine which didn't produce that much horsepower, were considered as history. If you know that, you

can understand why we developed the 928." These days, when vintage car shows and racing are quite popular, "We look at old Porsches in a much different way."

They certainly did in early 1992, when the design studios, which are located in Porsche's research center at Weissach, 25 kilometers west of Zuffenhausen, began sketching the proposed new midengine production car. Americans can take pride in the fact that one of the main designers beavering away behind those locked doors was one of their own. Initially assigned to the show car was Grant Larson, then a 34-year-old who was born in Billings, Montana, and grew up in Mequon, Wisconsin, just north of Milwaukee.

No new car is the result of just one designer's work. It's very much a team effort, but Lagaay explains: "Grant is a very important designer in the history of the concept car because he handed down many of the essential design elements. And then he put everything the show car had on the production version, which was a hard job."

Porsche designer Steve Murkett created this sketch of a roadster during the early stages of the development of the 986 program. At this point in the design process, many ideas were put forth as a theme was established for the new sports car. *Porsche AG*

GRANT LARSON

Twenty years before the exterior design of the Porsche Boxster proved his flair for designing automobiles, Grant Larson got his first job . . . dusting automobiles.

Larson grew up in Mequon, Wisconsin, not far from Milwaukee. One of the features of his hometown was the automobile museum of the famed designer, Brooks Stevens. For a kid infected with car fever, working in the museum was a natural.

Larson fondly remembers that job and Stevens' great automobiles, particularly, ". . . the Mercedes-Benz 540K roadster and, of course, the Figoni et Falaschi-bodied Talbot-Lago. I was too young to drive the cars, though I once got to move the 540K about 10 feet and got a big thrill out of it. I already loved cars and needed little nurturing, but I think the job gave me an understanding of shapes . . . rubbing my hands over the cars all the time. It was a very good experience and I graduated myself into the model shop and then as a design apprentice. Next, I discovered design schools.

"First, I went to the Milwaukee Institute of Art and Design. At the time, the Art Center in Pasadena seemed like too big a thing for a young Mequon kid, so I started slowly, studying industrial design for a while in Milwaukee, but one day realized that to meet my goals I was going to have to pack up and go the Art Center."

After graduating, Larson took a job at Audi's studio in Germany, which was then being run by another American, J. Mays, who is now director of Ford's worldwide design efforts. But when he had a chance to move to Porsche, Larson made the change, which put him in just the right place when the 986 project was initiated.

So where does a designer like Grant Larson get the inspiration to do a car like the Boxster?

"You can't really define it as saying I started out this way or that," Larson explains. "It's more like a collection of all the things you know or learned about cars ever since you were a kid. It starts with the first sports car—or the first Porsche—you ever saw. You collect all your best memories together, and it sort of happens.

"There are other things that influence you, too, right down to a funny little casting or machined piece you find in the garbage can. I tend to do that a lot at Porsche, digging through the scrap containers and taking little objects . . . they catch me doing that fairly often, but they just laugh."

Larson's life experiences with small imported cars—and Porsches—began "when I was really young. It was about 1963,

and my dad had a DKW Junior. I was five or six and my brother was two years older. He had a friend who lived around the corner and his father had a Porsche 356 coupe. We would compare cars and say things like, 'My dad's funny European car is better than your dad's funny European car.' I was always looking for reasons why my dad's DKW was neater than the Porsche . . . but eventually I thought, 'Come on, who am I trying to kid?'

"The Porsche was that mouse gray and the guy hardly ever took it out of the garage. It had the teardrop taillamps so it must have been from 1957 or later. I couldn't figure out why they would paint a car gray, and why this guy never drove the car. But the fact is that the very first sports car that ever took my attention was that old gray Porsche coupe."

Despite this long-time affinity for small European automobiles, Larson admits to also having a place in his heart for American muscle cars. When he was a teenager, his brother-in-law drove a Dodge Coronet R/T with a 440 Magnum V-8 and would take Larson and his friends for rides punctuated with burnouts. "That was heart throbbing at the time," Larson explains, "and it pulled me away from the small European cars for a while."

The designer reminds us: "Growing up in Wisconsin is, for the most part, Americana at its best. I was into huge tires, exhaust pipes hanging out, and injection stacks. My favorite car in the late 1960s was the 1968 Dodge Charger . . . and it's still a favorite. Of course," he adds, "tastes change as you grow older, though even cars like that remain influential."

His passion for Porsches made Larson one of the champions for a smaller model that would reflect images of the company's earlier cars. Naturally he can satisfy his interests in older Porsches with books and in the company's museum in Zuffenhausen, but Larson also once confided that "our favorite thing is the Oldtimer Grand Prix at the Nurburgring. I look forward to that every year. It's a fantastic race. We camp, drink beer, cook horrible sausages, and have a great time watching not only the Porsches, but everything." In the years they were working up to the Boxster he recalls, "There was a guy who would show up with a polished aluminum RSK or RS60, with the little headlamp covers. I photographed the heck out of the car . . . and it was always in the back of my mind."

This helps explain the inspiration that led to the Boxster. In a later conversation, Larson explained, "I had the Boxster show car in my mind from the first couple of sketches. There was something that just clicked. I knew how it should look and the show car went together relatively quickly. It just seemed logical and easy . . . it wasn't easy, of course, but it seemed like it was."

He also pays tribute to the design team at Porsche, adding, "I have to give credit to colleagues of mine, because as ideas flow through the studio, there's always this exchange between designers."

Larson recalls what it was like to watch the progress of the Boxster from sketches to clay models then to production. "There were these little milestones that took place along the way," he explains. "We were doing the clay models, pushing them back and forth. They must weigh about twice as much as a car and you have to be careful to not smear the clay.

"Then the clay model disappears for a few weeks and comes back as a 'see-through' fiberglass model that brings the exterior and interior together. Suddenly you think, 'It's almost a real car.' For the very first time you get a chance to sit behind the wheel and look out as if you could drive the car. You can say, 'So that's what that fender looks like from the driver's position.'

"The second milestone was during winter testing, just before Christmas, 1994. They were testing the very first running prototypes around the Weissach area. I got on the list to ride as a passenger with one of the test drivers. I met him at 6 A.M. for a five-hour drive down through the Black Forest . . . and that was a key moment for me. This was one of those nasty matte black test mule cars, but it's the very first time I could sit in the car when it was a running prototype.

"I couldn't get over how light the car felt. After pushing around the clay models and the fiberglass car, this one was propelled on its own. The first driving experiences were also like that, with the car feeling so light.

"It took a long time to finally see a car that was correct," he continues, "but what made the difference was when all the things are there, you begin to think of it as a real car. As accurate a representation as those first non-running cars might be, you're still not convinced. Then the first cars show up and you can see some bits and pieces from the underbody, little spoilers that pull in brake cooling air. Finally you see all the things that make it a real automobile."

Asked what he now thinks when he sees a production Boxster go by, Larson explains, "There's a sense of relief and

success, and also a good feeling that you made some owners really happy and fulfilled one of their dreams." He then echoes Harm Lagaay's attitude when he says he might also ". . . think of all the things I wish we could have continued working on or how we might have done something differently."

Larson also enjoys the fact that "Boxster owners don't leave their cars alone, which I think is perfectly okay and shows they are excited about them. If you don't care about your car, you just drive it. If you really care, you want to do little things that personalize it. I've seen owners in Germany who put little stickers on their spoiler so when it goes up it says something like 'Have a nice day' in English. People put on the tuning bits and pieces, like wheels and such, and above all, personalized license plates. You can't spell out words on German plates like you can in America, but they usually have '986' in there somewhere."

All of which must be quite gratifying for Larson, who now lives in Ludwigsburg, near Zuffenhausen, with his wife, Stefanie, and their two daughters, Paulina and Louisa. It's been quite a successful career for the "young Mequon kid," who dared to leave home to study at the world's best automotive design school, who retains a love for American muscle cars, and who enjoys digging through the scrap containers at Porsche.

Grant Larson, born in Montana and raised in Wisconsin, attended the famous Art Center College of Design in Pasadena, California. Moving to Europe to work in Audi's studio, he switched to Porsche and was given the job of creating the Boxster show car, which became the basis for the production version.

The two men responsible for much of the Boxster show car were Grant Larson (left) and interior designer Stefan Stark (right). Here the pair is seen visiting the 1994 Los Angeles Auto Show, where they give the thumbs up to the interior of a street rod.

Throughout the summer and into the autumn of 1992, there were the four possible production designs being developed in one studio while the show car was being worked on in another. Lagaay had Larson working on the show car. "I realized that the show car was the best car, so I put Grant on the production team. All the designers who had done other things were taken out and he had to do the 986 (the Boxster) alongside the 996 (the 911)."

Lagaay adds, "Grant is also a person who has always looked after that idea of having a smaller type of car with lots of Porsche heritage. He has always been thinking about that and fought for it and argued for it."

While Larson did the exterior of the show car, Lagaay points out, "I had an interior designer called Stefan Stark. The chief modeler who did most of the work and was able to interpret everything we were sketching and talking about was Peter Muller. Those were the three guys who did the shape of the show car."

Like any complex design project, the Boxster show car wasn't perfect from the start. "And what was wrong with it in the beginning," Lagaay remembers, "is that the proportions were wrong. The windshield was too high, the rear end was too short, and the wheelbase was too long. I kept on chopping until I thought the proportions were right. That's when the design theme came in, because the first Boxster show car design theme was not strong enough, it was too soft, it didn't have enough tension and so on. Gradually it got better and better."

While the 986 and 996 were being developed in one studio, the Boxster show car was under development next door. There was constant inspiration going back and forth

It was Porsche's RSKs and RS60s that inspired Grant Larson when he began his drawings for the Boxster show car. This photo was taken by Larson on one of the trips he made to vintage race car events in Germany. *Grant Larson*

between the two. Lagaay points out, "The packages of both cars (986 and Boxster show car) were not that far apart at the beginning, and it was only after a couple of months that we realized that the show car package would be too small as a production car. But we didn't change the show car; we went on with that but changed the package and the concept of the production version."

With the Boxster show car being readied for its debut in Detroit, the design team for the production Boxster was tackling the complex problem of fitting everything inside the exterior design. This is the difficult art of packaging an automobile, which was made more difficult with the Boxster because it was a totally new, clean-sheet-of-paper (or, more appropriately these days, a blank-computer-screen) project.

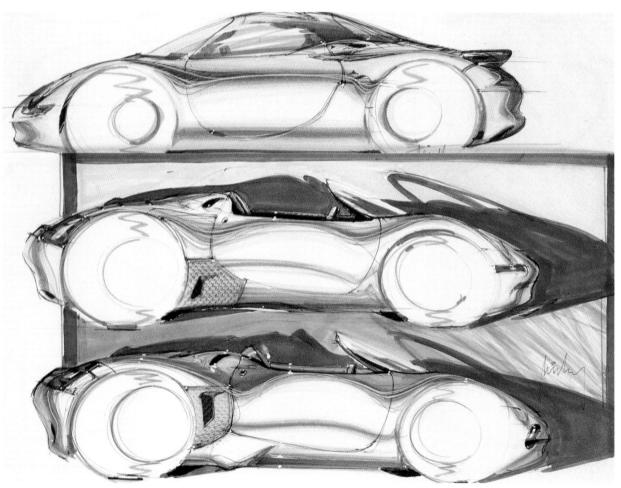

When a new car program begins, designers lay down the basic ideas and themes from which a production car can be developed. Pinky Lai of the Porsche studio sketched these ideas of where a 986 design might begin, creating forms and shapes from which a production car could be developed. *Porsche AG*

"Everything was new," Lagaay states emphatically. "You should realize there has never been a decent, midengine, soft-top sports car. You won't, for instance, find one in history with a decent soft top that easily goes up and down. That's what made it difficult, because everything was new . . . it was midengine and water cooled . . . the struts were too high . . . luggage space had to be there. And it all had to be right. I've designed many cars, but on this one everything was a problem because it was so new.

"Package-wise, it was the most difficult car I have ever done. As an example, you create a beautiful headlamp shape, so you draw in all the latest technology, and yet it has to be cost efficient because you can't have 300 versions for around the world, only 5. Then you realize you have this huge radiator underneath it, and the headlamp you want doesn't fit on top of the radiator . . ."

During his stint at BMW, Lagaay was responsible for that company's famous Z-1 limited-production sports car,

These sketches show the development of Grant Larson's ideas for the Boxster as they are developed from the first ideas and themes into a more rationalized shape that could be refined still more into a production car. *Porsche AG*

TAPE DRAWINGS

 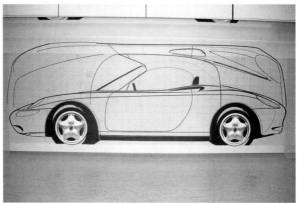

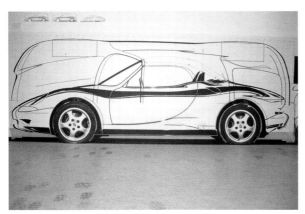 

These are "tape drawings" of major proposals for the Boxster done by (from left to right, top to bottom) Wolfgang Moebius, Matthias Kulla, Pinky Lai, and Steve Murkett. At this stage, the designs have been refined from original sketches and made "life-size" for evaluation in tape on a flat surface, represented as both side and overhead views. From this stage, approved design proposals could go to the clay model stage. *Porsche AG*

which Lagaay figures "was already one of the most extreme packages I'd done. The Boxster was more difficult than that . . . and more difficult than the 996 because of packaging. It's so tight. You need to have six-foot-tall people trying to fit in and yet there is this engine . . . so there were pulleys being moved back and forth as engineers tried to make the engine shorter so we could get tall people in the car."

Like any truly inspired executive, Lagaay didn't think of these as problems, but as challenges, the most difficult of which was "water cooling, because the radiators were so large by Porsche terms. We struggled. It was generally felt that the proportions of the car were not right because of the heavy front end caused by the radiators. But the reason was simple: the rest of the car was so agile and so elegant. Moving forward to the front axle we had this small car, and then we had this heavy front end with the radiators ahead of the front wheels. It never looked right. We had sleepless nights over that, but one day I said the only solution is to enlarge the rest of the car to the proportions of the front end. So in autumn 1993, I enlarged the whole car. And that was it. We never looked back.

"In actual fact," Lagaay suggests, "I think the radiator thing is a design and engineering accomplishment because it is so tight. From a thermodynamic point of view, no other company has done it in such a compact way."

Also tightly packaged in the Boxster's front end are its beautiful headlights, which go counter to traditional Porsche single-headlamp configuration. That makes the new headlights a bit controversial to some Porschephiles. Lagaay says, "The idea of going away from one single headlamp with all the other functions around it, and combining

Inside Porsche's design studio, the clay model of the Boxster production car goes through continual development as the final form of the car is carefully defined. Grant Larson (white shirt) consults with two modelers. *Porsche AG*

it all into one module was made way before the 986 and 996 prototypes and then adapted to the Boxster show car. We had all kinds of different headlamp designs in 1992, but decided on the type on the show car, though the production car's technology is quite different." He points out, "This is just the beginning of a revolution in lighting, because light is speed and speed is light and the better light you have, the faster you can go."

The design challenges continued. "Like how do you create such different characters for the 986 and 996 with so many parts being the same? I think that if you were to write down today that 40 percent of the two cars should be the same, you would possibly say it can't be done. But as you see, it can be done. There will always be people who will say, 'On principle I don't like the idea of having the same parts,' but I think they will get used to it."

Naturally, however, this sharing of parts did cause difficulties. Like the doors, which are the same for both the 986 and 996. One of the important design themes in the Boxster concept car, however, involved the rear fenders and how they flowed out of the doors. The problem was that the same theme (and doors) couldn't be used for the 911. Lagaay says it was "like two people dancing together and one wants to do the cha-cha and one wants to do the tango. It was so difficult to have those two themes come out of the same door and that was really a nightmare.

"In the end, we solved it by having the door be very subtle, with a big shoulder, but no hard theme so that whenever the door starts you can make a Boxster out of it or you can make a 911 out of it. And the future will show that it works, because we have derivatives coming from this . . ." (though he refused to elaborate on those derivatives).

Incidentally, the two cars also have the same front fenders, hood, and outside rearview mirrors.

There were times when designing the Boxster and 911 in parallel got a bit tricky, because they shared many components and were aimed at similar but not identical market segments. Lagaay gets a small smile on his face and explains, "Obviously one of the times when the air was full of tension was when the two design teams, one working on the 996, one on the Boxster, met each other. And I was the referee.

"That went on for quite a long time until I said, 'Do you know how it's going to be? It's going to be how I want it.' And they almost felt some relief." And Lagaay knows why, because he's been down that road himself. "I've been involved in so many design projects with my heart, and everything I heard that was said about my car went right to my heart. I know how designers feel when I say I want it this way or that way. On the other hand, I have distance and it doesn't hurt when I change something, and since they know that they say, 'Okay, fair enough, if you say so there's probably something right about that.' "

The Boxster design team also had to wrestle with the car's aerodynamics, though the problem was not about trying to achieve a low coefficient of drag (Cd). Lagaay says it was ". . . about getting past the old fashioned notion of looking at a car and saying, 'You need a very high rear end for your typical good Cd factors.' Today we know you can achieve good figures in other ways. With the underbody. With tweaks here and there . . . and now we have very good figures both in lift and Cd." As it turned out, the smooth underbody floor pan lowered the car's overall drag coefficient by some 6 percent and the lift on the front axle by an impressive 36 percent.

At 0.31 with the top up, the Boxster's Cd is the best of any small roadster, and better than Porsche anticipated at the beginning of aero development. But it wasn't easy. "There were days in the beginning," he admits, "when we had lift like crazy in the back." But then he goes back into history and recalls, "There were also days when people said you can never get a 911 rear end aerodynamically right. Then it became the first car with the moving spoiler; that was a big step in terms of aerodynamics. The next version was better because the underbody was working for it. And the 996 is better still. Even the aerodynamicists had to change their perspective, because everything

At one point the Boxster show car was done up as a race car, but it turned out to be only a tease, as the factory has said it will never enter the car in competition, leaving that task to its 911 models. *Porsche AG*

from the B-pillar rearward underneath the car has an enormous influence on lift." Lagaay explains that you need a lot more time to develop the under-car aerodynamics, but adds, "The results are sensational."

As for the aero of the upper side of the Boxster, "We talked with the aerodynamicists for ages to persuade them to find other ways than just using a big spoiler, because we had spoilers . . . you cannot believe it . . . we had soft rear ends and big lips on them. I said, 'You can't do that, you have to have a moving device.' Naturally they were against every moving device because it costs money. But we settled on this spoiler that hardly sticks out—even less so in America because of the speeds—and can be shut off if you like." An owner can also manually deploy the spoiler, but it doesn't come up automatically to lower drag and lift on its own until the car is at 75 miles per hour, and sinks back into the bodywork once you're below 50 miles per hour.

There were discussions over the shape of the Boxster's tail end that covered more than the matter of aerodynamics. Lagaay recounts, "One of the big challenges for me was that despite the success of the show car, there were lots of people, even among the board of directors, who believed that type of rear end is not modern enough . . . and I had to fight like crazy for it."

When all the aerodynamic work was finished, the Boxster's numbers were impressive. Matching the drag coefficient of 0.31 with a frontal area of 1.93 square meters gives the sports car an overall aerodynamic drag number of 0.59. Lift on the front and rear of the car is almost the same, measuring 0.13/0.10.

"And then there was the challenge of not having enough luggage space. We knew one thing: 50 percent of our owners play golf. And where you do carry your golf bag? But we packaged it in a way that there's more space in the rear of a Boxster than there is in the coupe. You can get your golf bag in the back of a coupe, but it's not as easy as in a Boxster."

Also on the list of Boxster challenges: the windshield. And Lagaay shows the sort of passion designers bring to

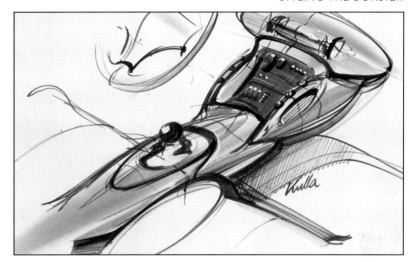

Matthias Kulla, who played a part in the final design of the Boxster interior, including the overlapping of the three instruments, did this interior design proposal sketch. *Porsche AG*

their craft: "They wanted a high windshield and I said, 'You can't do that on this type of car, you need a low windshield.'

"But they said, 'You can't see the stoplights.'

"I said, 'The hell with the stoplights. The people who buy a Boxster will always live with that. So what? That's the pain you like.'"

Looking to the inside of the Boxster, Lagaay recalls when the project began in early 1992, saying, "In those days, we still had three to four months between the start of the exterior design and beginning the interior design. These days we would begin at the same time. Back then, we felt we had to have the periphery, where the shoulder of the door is, the belt line, the windscreen, the A-pillar, and we waited until we'd fixed these to start on the interior. Today we'd think that was a waste of time."

The theme of Stefan Stark's interior for the Boxster show car did influence the production car, although they also had other proposals. One added design was from the studio's own Steve Murkett, with another done outside Porsche by an Italian studio.

Grant Larson, who gets credit for the Boxster's exterior, will tell you that designing the interior is a more difficult assignment, explaining, "The interior is like a collec-

tion of products that have to work well with each other. It requires a lot more concentration and attention."

While the show car had five instruments, which is considered a trademark of the 911, the Boxster's gauges were consolidated into three. Nonetheless, the two cars do share something of the same overall theme because they

Designer Pinky Lai's Boxster proposal carried over the traditional Porsche single headlamp design with the turn signals in the bumper. Porsche's chief designer, Harm Lagaay, points out, ". . . this is a softer theme and a very distinctive rear air inlet. The door shut lines are not so dramatic as on the production car."

use some of same pieces and the structure under the instrument pod. And there's even a historical tie for the Boxster's gauge layout because the race car that inspired its exterior theme, the RSK, also had three dials.

While the Boxster show car had a light background for its instruments, the production car reverts to the classic white-on-black dials. You can special-order light-colored gauges from Porsche, but, Lagaay points out, "We feel they just aren't practical enough. There are moments early in the morning before dawn that you can't read them. We are a very practical kind of people. . . ."

Among the features retained from Stark's show car design is the little bridge across the top of the instrument panel that lets a little light peek through.

The pull bar on the door panel, which was an aluminum extrusion on the show car, was kept on the production version, where it's molded into the door panel. Naturally the many individual ventilation fans had to be removed, and covers were added over the pockets in the doors. Originally the Boxster was going to have an even

The rear view of Pinky Lai's version shows a higher rear end than the final version, even with a hint of the 944/968 cabriolet. This taller tail wasn't for added luggage space but for aerodynamic reasons as Porsche was still trying to use a built-in spoiler rather than one that rose out of the back of the car. Once the decision was made that a powered, rising spoiler could be used for high-speed stability, designers were able to lower the bodywork to the softer shape used on the production 986. The little slit at the back of the deck lid included the high-mounted rear stoplight. Note that this version had dual exhausts.

Wolfgang Moebius' Boxster design has a softer front end with, like Pinky Lai's design, a center air intake for the radiators, showing the difficult radiator packaging problems had yet to be tackled. Again a single headlamp is used, this time with a more distinctive turn signal in the bumper. At this point—late June 1992—the designs had a short front overhang. This had to be lengthened when the two front radiators were added, but also to increase crash crush space and luggage capacity in the Boxster's sister car, the 911, with which it shares its basic nose structure.

simpler door panel—trying to retain a simple roadster feel—with no cover on the cubby hole. Designer Steve Murkett explains, "Your arm would lie on the edge between the tube and the door surface. And it worked reasonably well, but we found it was possible for people with thinner arms to feel a bit like they were going to fall in the hole, so we ended up putting a little cover on it."

Among the pieces of equipment integrated into the Boxster design is the heating/ventilation/air conditioning (HVAC) control panel, which owners of the Audi A4 might recognize, though with a new pictograph panel. Insisting on its own specific HVAC system would have been very expensive for Porsche and, as one observer pointed out, the chosen system is very effective in a small car like the Boxster.

Again the rear end shows an attempt at a rear spoiler that was part of the bodywork. That is not, incidentally, an odd half-spoiler, but this clay model was shared by Moebius and Grant Larson, each of whom used one side of the car. Note the softer fender shape than on the Boxster show car, and the lack of a side air intake. There was concern that such an inlet would not be considered Porsche-like and would look a bit too much like an imitation of Ferrari. But once the Boxster package was established, Porsche found the inlets worked very nicely from an aerodynamic standpoint and so used the small intakes. These openings also filled the sheet-metal area to the rear of the doors. While those doors had a good shut line for the 911 (which shares doors with the Boxster), they created a long, empty space aft of the doors in the midengine Boxster. The intakes also visually differentiate the midengine 986 Boxster from the rear-engine 996 911, which has no side intakes.

In this version of Grant Larson's early Boxster proposal, you can already see influences of the show car. There is still a central air intake and the headlamps are beginning to take on the look of the final car. The light's various functions—main beam, dip beam, fog lamp, blinker, and washer jets—were later integrated into one modular unit, which is easier to install and maintain. At one point, the Boxster and 911 shared the same windscreen, but it was decided that the glass was too tall for the roadster. One of the reasons for the high rear deck on this and the Moebius' design (which shares the same clay model) is that designers were still dealing with a conventional folding soft top because the unique, compact, "Z-movement" mechanism had yet to be considered. *Porsche AG*

Porsche owners would have no trouble recognizing the seats in the Boxster, which borrow from the classic 911 shape. Designer Grant Larson points out, "If you've got something good going, don't wander away from it. Porsche seats have always been very good and there's no reason to head off in a different direction, therefore we kept things the same. We just adjusted things like the stitching pattern and added new leather colors."

One feature held over from the Boxster show car to production was the brick red of that car's leather uphol-stery as one interior color choice. However, the idea of having different seats for the driver and passenger couldn't be kept for practical reasons. Not only is it an expensive idea, but it would make producing both left- and right-hand drive vehicles difficult. Maybe we get a look to the future when Harm Lagaay comments, "I think one of the things that's wrong about cars today is that the passenger's seat is exactly the same as the driver's."

While a close look at the Boxster and 911 instru-ment panels and seats will bring some obvious compar-

isons, the overall image of the two interiors is quite different. Not only is the Boxster a definite two-seater versus the generous 2+2 layout of the 911, but there are also differences in how the interior surfaces are finished that separate the two.

Now you might think that given the Boxster's interior and exterior and all the positive comments made about the car since its debut, Porsche design director, Harm Lagaay, might bask in all that glory. And you'd be wrong.

When he sees a Boxster on the road, "It's always the

Still closer to its final form, the Grant Larson Boxster in clay form shows slight differences in the nose intakes, the rear engine inlets and rollover hoops, elements that were changed before the car went into production. *Porsche AG*

same reaction," he says. "I look at all the mistakes and try to find the solutions."

That isn't the comment of a malcontent, just a perfectionist who continues to learn and refine his art. "It takes a minimum of a couple of years before you settle down with a design," he explains. "This can happen with many creative disciplines, but with cars it's more drastic, because it's a lot of money going into a project and you can only learn from the things you reconsider. We don't have mistakes, but we have imperfections—it's important to learn and the next time you take all the things you've learned, fold them into the new project, and it gets better and better. There are also things you might think are not all that great, but after a few years you look at it and notice that it does add character to the car. And that's okay."

CHAPTER FIVE

POWER TO THE PORSCHE

It was always the sound that made the difference. With your foot flat on the floor, the car taking a slight squat under acceleration, there was something comforting about that typical Porsche air-cooled sound behind you. Whether a bit raspy in a four-cylinder 356 or slightly smoother in a 911, that wonderful noise was the signature that let you know you were in one of Zuffenhausen's finest. Guaranteed fun.

And yet in the mid-1970s, Porsche was giving us the distinct impression it was all over. Air-cooled boxer engines had been a grand tradition, carrying Porsche through its early 356 days and for more than a decade of 911s that became more powerful despite modern antipollution laws. But those evermore stringent regulations would spell the death of the air-cooled flat-six, they said. Future Porsches—924s and the upcoming 928—would need to be water-cooled, while packaging considerations favored a front engine that wouldn't be flat.

All this made sense to the engineers and many journalists, but it was unacceptable to the most important audience of all: Porsche buyers. No matter how quick, fun, and modern the front-engine Porsches became, they just weren't the same. They were Porsches all right, complete with the badge, but they were, well, not different enough from the rest of the crowd.

So when the Boxster and 911 development teams began to lay down the specifications for this new pair of Porsches, there was only momentary doubt the engines would be flat and fitted behind the cockpit. Apparently there was a brief discussion about fitting the Audi V-6 amidships, but that possibility was quickly discarded to maintain tradition.

There would have to be one concession to modernity. Air cooling had to go, but by the time development of the engines began in early 1992, Porsche already had a rich history of victorious race cars with boxer engines equipped with water-cooled cylinder heads. A similar system was

In creating the Boxster, Porsche designed an all-new flat-six engine, which shares only such basics as layout and bore centers with its predecessor. In addition to water cooling, other changes include four valves per cylinder and an internal dry sump oiling system. *Porsche AG*

Aluminum is used for the block and cylinder heads of the new Boxster powerplant. Assembled in Porsche's Werk 2 factory, the new engine produces 201 horsepower at 6,000 rpm and 181 lb.-ft. of torque at 4,500 rpm. *Porsche AG*

also used on one production flat-six, the twin-turbo version fitted to the famous four-wheel-drive 959.

So what do the new engines share with the traditional Porsche powerplant? Six cylinders and the fact they are laid out in the classic "boxer" design. Inherited from VW and used by companies as varied as Alfa Romeo and Subaru, this configuration gets its nickname from the fact the cylinders

lie flat in opposed banks. The pistons move in and out attached to a crankshaft mounted between the cylinders. It's this outward punching motion that leads to the "boxer" tag. The advantages of this design tend to be the ability to package the engine low in a chassis and a lower center of gravity.

Also carried over from the previous flat-six are the new engine's bore centers. This tends to be a tradition in famous engines. When Chevrolet redesigned its small block V-8 and retained its classic bore centers, one of its engineers pointed out there are only a few constants in nature, but they include the speed of light and the bore centers of the Chevrolet V-8—and the bore centers of Porsche's flat-six. In the six, this carryover measurement is 118 millimeters (4.65 inches) between the centers of each bank's cylinders. Retaining this measurement also has a practical side, like being able to make the new engines on the same equipment as the old sixes.

Porsche also carried over its philosophy of a short-stroke engine. The flat-six's 2,480 cc of engine displacement comes in the form of an 85.5-millimeter (3.37-inch) bore and 72.0-millimeter (2.83-inch) stroke. These "over-square" measurements are considered best for the expected combination of power, high rpm, and smoothness.

And that was about all Porsche carried over from its classic powerplant.

What's new? It begins with the cylinder block, which is cast—like much of the engine—in aluminum. It's a two-

One of the problems with a midengine design is keeping interior noise to a minimum because the powerplant is so close to the passenger compartment. Here you can see just how close it is in the Boxster, but despite this the noise level is no more than in other sports cars. *Porsche AG*

piece casting, split vertically and bolted together to create the block. Fitted between the block halves is a forged steel crankshaft that has 12 counterweights and spins in seven main bearings that are in gray cast-iron inserts in an aluminum bearing case.

Attached to the crankshaft are cast-aluminum pistons that have a thin iron coating to ensure long life as the they slide back and forth along the cylinder bores. And those pistons slide on a surface with a thin coating of silicon that reduces wear on the cylinder walls and piston rings.

Like most modern automakers, Porsche uses "cracked" connecting rods to attach its pistons to the crankshaft. Tra-

One of the packaging problems with the Boxster was providing sufficient interior room and then fitting the entire drivetrain package, including the exhaust system, in the back. A major engineering goal involved acoustics, making certain the water-cooled Boxster flat-six sounded like a classic air-cooled Porsche. *Porsche AG*

ditionally, connecting rods were made in two pieces, the largest being the rod and the upper C-shaped half of its "big end" to which it is attached to the crankshaft. The smaller piece is the similarly C-shaped other half of the big end. These two halves are bolted together to attach the rod to the crankshaft. To be properly assembled, the halves of the rod big end must have precisely machined faces so they fit tightly when assembled, but even then they are just that: two pieces joined by a bolt.

Porsche's "cracked" rods are forged in steel as one piece. A laser beam precisely scores a point halfway down the circle of the big end. The end is then frozen to make it more brittle, pulled apart and it splits—actually cracking with a sound that will make you jump—at the scored point. The rod's big end is now in two pieces. Unlike the smooth machined surfaces of the two pieces that are joined in the traditional manner, these are rough to the touch. And yet when joined and bolted together, they merge, almost like one solid piece.

Oiling for the Boxster six is by Porsche's traditional dry sump, though in a rather untraditional manner. Usually a dry sump system has a separate tank from which the oil is cycled to the engine, circulated, picked up, cooled, and pumped back to the tank. The advantages of this system are a ready supply of oil and a low engine profile, as there's no need for a deep sump to hold the needed supply of lubricant.

For its new engine, Porsche developed what it calls "integrated dry-sump lubrication." The principle is unchanged, but simplified with the "tank" for the oil integrated into the block, but separated from the area of the crankshaft. This design eliminates the need for the separate tank and the hoses needed to connect the two.

Housed in its tank, which is baffled to prevent it from sloshing around, the oil is drawn off by a pump at the front of the engine and circulated where needed in the engine. A pair of scavenger pumps pick up the oil that has been moved through the engine and send it back to the oil reserve where it is stored until needed again.

In place of the traditional external oil cooler, the Boxster engine has an oil/coolant heat exchanger. When the engine is first started, the oil is warmed by the coolant, so it more quickly reaches its proper operating temperature. Likewise, when the oil becomes hotter than the coolant—which is about 90 degrees Celsius—the oil temperature is lowered by the coolant.

Cooling for the entire engine is, of course, the biggest change for the flat-six. Drawing on its racing experience, Porsche uses a cross-flow pattern that sends the coolant around the cylinders and combustion chambers in an open-deck design. One of the objectives is to make certain all the cylinders are working at the same temperature so that combustion is not just complete, but also consistent, which is important for holding down emissions. So coolant is pumped from the exhaust side to the intake side, routed around the working parts of the engine to evenly dissipate heat, and then back to the radiator.

Like the engine block, the cylinder heads, camshaft housing, and their covers are cast in aluminum. They are identical for the two banks of cylinders, so the heads could be swapped, all the better to save a bit of money. In another move to save a production step and eliminate possible errors, the oiling routes are cast in, so later drilling and cleaning are unnecessary.

One of the several advantages of water cooling the engine is the ability to use four valves per cylinder, the first time such a layout has been designed into the company's regular production flat-six. With water cooling, the extra heat generated by this design can be dissipated.

The four valves are fitted in each cylinder's compact penta-roof design and opened by a pair of chain-driven camshafts, one each for the intake and exhaust cams. The valves are opened by way of cup tappets and closed via conical springs. With automatic hydraulic adjustment for the valves, and an automatic tensioner for the chains, Porsche figures the valvetrain requires no maintenance.

Located in the roof of each combustion chamber, smack in the middle of the valves, is a single spark plug.

Although topside access to the Boxster's flat-six is difficult, Porsche claims normal maintenance can be performed from underneath the sports car. In this photo, you can also get a sense of the flat underbody of the Boxster, which led to good aerodynamics.

Since Porsche employs a cross-flow pattern for the air-fuel mixture though the chamber, it feels it needs only that one plug per cylinder.

Timing of the 12 intake valves is changeable, thanks to Porsche's VarioCam system. Start the engine and the intake valves are retarded 12.5 degrees, all the better to keep hydrocarbon emissions down. When the flat-six is revved above 1,200 rpm, a piston acting in the chain that opens the intake valves changes the timing so the intake is advanced 12.5 degrees. With the intakes opening earlier, more air-fuel mixture is drawn into the combustion chambers. As a result, each chamber is more completely filled with the mixture and with that comes added low-end torque with little rise in hydrocarbon emissions. Take the engine above 5,120 rpm and VarioCam reverses the timing chain-piston's action for cruising, smoothing engine operation and again inhibiting hydrocarbons.

Distribution of the fuel is by way of a Bosch Motronic M 5.2 engine management system. Electronics read the airflow through a hot-film air mass metering system that is inside the air filter housing. Air then flows through a central throttle housing, its flow being controlled by a main throttle butterfly valve. The air being drawn to the combustion chambers gets there by way of a lightweight plastic intake manifold. The inner surfaces of the intake runners are quite smooth, as though they were polished metal intake runners, all the better to aid airflow.

At the same time, sensors in the exhaust system are reading the amount of oxygen at the other end of the combustion process. Matching that reading with the incoming airflow, the electronics precisely control the flow of fuel to each cylinder's injector. The same electronics fire the spark plugs, each of which has its own ignition coil.

Once burned, the mixture flows out past the exhaust valves and into a stainless-steel exhaust manifold. From there it is dumped into a catalytic converter and then the muffler, after which it exits through a wonderful little reminder of Porsche's RSK days. As on the Boxster concept car, the production 986 has a single central exhaust outlet in its lower rear valance panel. That central exhaust helped engineers keep something even more important than this visual tie to older Porsches: the sound of the flat-six's exhaust. Without that classic noise, the Boxster would have been missing an important part of its heritage. So along with physically packaging all the exhaust components tightly into the back of the sports car, engineers had a serious acoustic goal, which was to keep that traditional sound despite continually tougher exhaust noise requirements. Porsche's rear-mounted engines already make these checks difficult because unlike a front-engine car, both the engine compartment and exhaust noises are on the same end of the car. As it happens, using the center exhaust outlet aids a bit in meeting the noise rules because of the manner in which the sound-recording microphones are placed during the test.

One tradition Porsche couldn't retain for the Boxster was the time-honored act of showing off your new car's engine to admiring friends. In locating the engine amidships, putting

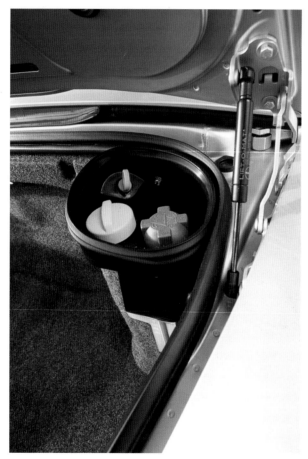

The driver can do simple maintenance by way of the far right corner of the rear luggage area. You can check the coolant level via the expansion tank sight level, and add coolant by removing the blue cover. You check the oil level with the yellow-handled dipstick, adding oil under the yellow cap.

Porsche designed the five-speed manual gearbox for the Boxster in cooperation with Volkswagen. One of the few complaints with the Porsche roadster is the vagueness of the cable-operated shifter for the manual transmission. *Porsche AG*

a generous trunk behind it, and then designing a top that would fold completely away in a compact top stack above the flat-six, there was no way also to provide a traditional engine cover. If you *really* want to show off your engine, you partially raise the top, disconnect its trailing edge, undo a few simple fasteners, and lift off a panel that exposes the top of the powerplant. Total time? About eight minutes with a little practice.

In addition to the packaging explanation, Porsche also points out that it has laid out the engine compartment so that all normal maintenance can be done from under the car. Modern electronic systems do away with much of the traditional maintenance, and their functions can be checked through computers. Spark plugs and oil filters, which need changing only every 30,000 miles, can be reached from beneath. It's only at 120,000 miles, when

The source of the Boxster's Tiptronic automatic transmission is the famous German firm ZF. With five speeds, the transmission can be driven like a traditional automatic with the shifter in "D." Optionally, the driver can shift gears via buttons on the steering wheel, a la Formula 1 cars. *Porsche AG*

you need to replace the self-adjusting poly-rib belt that serpentines around the front of the engine to drive such accessory items as air conditioning compressor and the power steering pump, that the mechanic even needs to remove the engine access panel. The few things the owner needs (and, by the way, wants) to do, like checking fluid levels, can be accomplished from the front and rear luggage compartments.

In fact, Porsche rear-engine compartments haven't really been all that interesting to look at since the days when fuel injection took over from carburetors. Unlike, for instance, a Ferrari or Corvette, there hasn't been much engine to see under a Porsche lid, with just pulleys, fans, and—in the case of the turbos—intercoolers being the main visual features.

Assembled in Zuffenhausen's Werk 2, the completed Boxster engine weighs in at 402 pounds and has 72 fewer parts than the old two-valve engine. The first stop for the engine after assembly is a dynamometer on which it is run in for 30 minutes to test it for emissions and power. The latter should read out at 201 horsepower at 6,000 rpm and 181 pound-foot of torque at 4,500. As with many modern engines, that torque peak isn't as impressive as the shape of the torque curve, which really looks more like one of the Monument Valley's tabletop mesas. By just 1,750 rpm, three-quarters of that torque is already being developed, and it doesn't slip back down past that level until revs are at 6,500, just 200 rpm short of the redline.

Those peak engine power ratings, incidentally, require that the engine be run on unleaded premium gasoline. If that grade isn't available, the Boxster will run on lesser grades of fuel. The electronic engine management system can read the preignition knocking that comes with regular fuel and retard the ignition to prevent the knock, though this also lowers power a bit.

Matched to the flat-six is either of two transmissions. Traditionalists insist, of course, on a manual gearbox. The five-speed in the Boxster is done in conjunction with Volkswagen. Shifted by way of a tensioned cable, the five

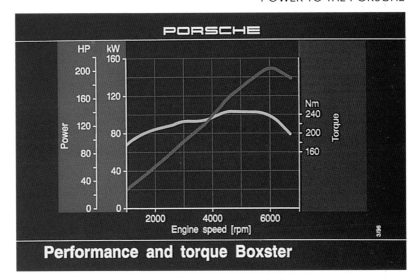

Power curves of the Boxster 2.5-liter flat-six show the maximum of 201 horsepower, which peaks at 6,000 rpm. Note the white, flat torque curve, which tops out at 4,500 rpm, but actually doesn't curve all that much, developing three-quarters of its 181 lb.-ft. by 1,750 rpm. *Porsche AG*

speeds are laid out in the pattern that has the normal H for 1-2-3-4, with 5th on a dogleg to the upper right. Reverse is below that, but there's little chance you might grab it accidentally as you have to go to neutral before moving the lever to the right and down to get the gear.

Clutch actuation is by way of hydraulics and through a two-piece flywheel that helps damp driveline vibrations. The other half of that combination is a single-plate dry clutch.

Not-so-traditionalists might opt for the Tiptronic automatic transmission, with its link to Formula 1 racing. This gearbox, which Porsche gets from ZF, now has five gears.

You can drive the Tiptronic conventionally, with the lever in "D" and no further shifting thought is needed on

PORSCHE BOXSTER

A nice visual and mechanical tie between the Boxster and the RSK-RS60 race cars is this center exhaust. The middle outlet also helps a bit in keeping exhaust noise down in noise-pollution tests, which are already difficult for Porsche because unlike front-engine vehicles, both its engine and exhaust are in back.

the driver's part. The transmission, however, is "thinking." The electronics that control shifting have five "maps" which contain different parameters, such as shift points and firmness or softness. Through a series of sensors that read inputs regarding throttle position, car and engine speed, and both acceleration and cornering forces, the transmission will opt for the map that best suits how the car is being driven. Cruise along calmly in traffic and the shifts will be smooth and in those areas of the power band that lead to comfortable driving. Start hauling down a twisting road, going for speed, and the gearbox will opt for a map that provides quick, crisp shifts that take maximum advantage of the power curves for best acceleration.

If you're *really* hauling down the road, looking for max performance, you'll probably nudge the shift lever to the left into "M." Now the Tiptronic is, for the most part, under your control. Shifts are made with buttons on the steering wheel, a la Formula 1 race cars. Push the "+" button and you'll go up a gear. Tag the "-" button and you'll quickly be down a gear.

Probably. Knowing we're all human, Porsche fits a few "cover your butt" features to the Tiptronic. It will not, for instance, activate the "-" push if it means revving the engine above its redline and risking damage. Punch in a

"+" while cornering and the gearbox won't make the shift until you've straightened out, all the better to prevent a chassis imbalance at the worst possible time. The Tiptronic even knows enough to change your shift points if you are going up or down hill, or to trim back on timing just a touch during shifting to smooth those shifts.

Under full acceleration, there are two additional aids for the driver. One is called ABD (Automatic Brake Differential), which is the equivalent of a limited-slip differential that offers up to 100 percent locking. Also helping watch your back is the (optional) traction control system. Should a wheel begin to spin, the anti-lock brake on just that wheel will slow it to help retain chassis balance.

That's the drivetrain package that powers the Boxsters: a traditional layout mixed with smooth acceleration and the expected Porsche engine sound. Match the flat-six with the manual and Porsche figures you'll get to 60 miles per hour in 6.7 seconds. Opt for the Tiptronic and they claim 7.4 seconds to the same speed.

Magazine road tests have shown the factory numbers to be rather conservative. *Road & Track* magazine, for instance, got a Boxster to 60 miles per hour in 6.1 seconds, beating Mercedes-Benz' supercharged SLK by 0.5 second and BMW's 6-cylinder Z3 by 0.4 second.

Good fun and bragging rights. A great combination.

CHAPTER SIX

BENEATH THE PRETTY FACE

For all the time spent on the Boxster in the design studios, an equal amount of effort was being spent under the skin. That was the job of the engineers who design the metal structure under the skin, the part you never see, but the equally artful design work that makes certain you enjoy your car, but also protects if you have the bad luck to be in an accident.

First, the fun part.

Using their computers, the engineers at Porsche were able to create a body that not only holds up well in accidents but also provides a solid platform to which the suspension and steering can be attached. The basic material in the Boxster body is steel, which is hot galvanized on both sides. With the 26-step process in which the body is prepped and painted, Porsche is able to offer a 10-year warranty against "rust through."

Despite all the steel used in the Boxster's body, some 20 percent of the car's overall weight of 2,756 pounds is aluminum, and that includes much of what goes into the handling part of the car.

With the Boxster body shape having as its inspiration such cars as the RSK, RS60, and 550 Spyder, it isn't surprising to find that it also shares a midengine layout with those models, decades of other successful Porsche race cars, the first postwar Porsche sports car—the 1948 356-001 prototype—and three-and-a-half decades of Formula 1 machines.

A midengine car design brings with it difficulties, as in the area of packaging. Where do you put the folded top? What about cooling? How much luggage space can you devise? But this sort of design also has some decided advantages in handling. The more you can locate the engine mass inside the wheelbase of a car, the more you can lower the polar moment of inertia around the car's vertical axis. With this comes such advantages as better weight balance and more responsive steering.

To take advantage of this weight balance and distribution advantage, the Boxster has MacPherson strut-based front and rear independent suspensions that are quite similar in design. The front suspension is mounted on a subframe,

Both the engineering and styling departments at Porsche will tell you the most difficult part of designing the Boxster was fitting all the necessary pieces in the design. Here that packaging problem can be seen in a cutaway Boxster, from the engine nestled up behind the cockpit to the angled radiators in the nose. *Porsche AG*

the rear on a transverse structure—both done in aluminum—and both use the same sort of struts, which contain conical springs and twin-tube gas-pressurized shock absorbers. Die-cast-aluminum wheel carriers hold, among other things, the wheel bearings and brakes. At the front, the wheels are located by lower A-arms, while the rear wheels each have a pair of lower lateral links and a single trailing link on each side.

Another feature of the Boxster suspension is the newest variation on the Weissach axle first seen on the 928. And it takes us another step away from the time when lifting off the gas and/or touching the brakes in a Porsche while cornering could be, well, best left to an expert. In this latest form of the elastokinematic design, when you turn into a corner with a Boxster, the outside front tire takes a slight negative toe attitude, while the outside rear has a positive toe position. If you increase your cornering

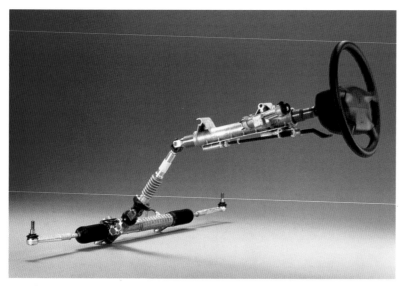

Rack-and-pinion steering with hydraulic servo assist is part of the Boxster chassis; with an overall ratio of 16.9:1, the system has 3.0 turns lock to lock. *Porsche AG*

speed, this design leads to more understeer and stability, making it possible in an emergency to lift off the gas or even dab at the brakes without assuming you will soon be kissing the guardrail.

Anti-sway bars are used fore and aft, the fronts measuring 23.1 millimeters and the rears 18.5 millimeters. If you're willing to trade some ride comfort for still flatter cornering, Porsche offers a Sport Suspension package that ups the anti-sway bar diameters to 23.6 millimeters front and 19.6 millimeters rear, to go with firmer shocks and springs, plus larger wheels and tires.

The brakes on those aluminum wheel carriers are backed by Porsche's many years of racing experience. They are based on a "mono-block" aluminum caliper that is said to reduce the chance of brake fade, and contains four pistons of different sizes to get even disc pad wear. Those pistons clamp their pads onto discs that measure 298 millimeters across and 24 millimeters thick at the front and 292 millimeters across and 20 millimeters thick at the back. The emergency brake has a cable-operated drum (164-millimeter diameter, 20 millimeters wide) on the rear axle. Naturally the Boxster has anti-lock brakes, using Bosch's ABS 5.3 system.

Steering is by power-assisted rack and pinion, the rack being hollow to save still more weight. The ratio of the steering is 16.9:1 with 2.85 turns lock to lock.

Then there are elements of the chassis that are, for some drivers, as important for its looks as for its function: wheels and tires. Standard are 205/55ZR-16s on 6.0x16-inch alloy wheels up front, the rears being 225/50ZR-16s on 7.0x16-inch alloys. Opt for the Sport Suspension and the tires get a bit larger and squattier, with the fronts going up to 205/50Z-17s on 7.0x17-inch alloys and the rears to 225/40ZR-17s on 8.5x17s.

More important to many owners than the size is that the wheels and tires look good, so Porsche offers two optional alloy wheels and the choice of Conti or Pirelli tires. Regardless of size, what makes a difference on the Boxster is that the various designers and engineers made

Left

The Boxster's front suspension is mounted on the car's subframe and is based on MacPherson struts located by lower A-arms. In the struts are conical springs and twin-tube gas-pressurized shock absorbers. *Porsche AG*

Below

The rear suspension is mounted on a transverse aluminum subframe that doubles as reinforcement for the rear end. Similar to the front suspension, the rear design is also based on MacPherson struts but located by lower lateral arms and trailing links. *Porsche AG*

Basic Boxster wheels are of 16-inch diameter, made of aluminum alloy and measure 6.0 inches across for the fronts and 7.0 inches for the rears. The extra-cost Sport Suspension ups the diameter to 17 inches and the widths to 7.0 inches front and 8.5 inches rear.

Left
Relying on its racing experience, Porsche designed the Boxster's four-wheel disc brakes with mono-block aluminum calipers that have four pistons of various size to get more equal brake pad wear. Cooling air for the front discs is routed to them via front ducts and suspension-mounted deflectors. Bosch ABS is part of the brake system. *Porsche AG*

certain the wheels and tires fill the wheelwells in such a manner that they give a car a solid stance—both mechanically and visually—on the road.

Wheels and tires are also one of the few easily seen elements created during the thousands of hours during which body and chassis engineers beavered away in front of their computer screens, ground away still more laps on test tracks,

and watched as early prototypes were destroyed in crash tests.

Naturally, safety was of great importance in designing the Boxster, and the better automakers approach this important subject from two angles: active and passive. The former is all the things the engineers do to keep you out of an accident in the first place. This includes such attributes as a high level of predictable handling, excellent brakes,

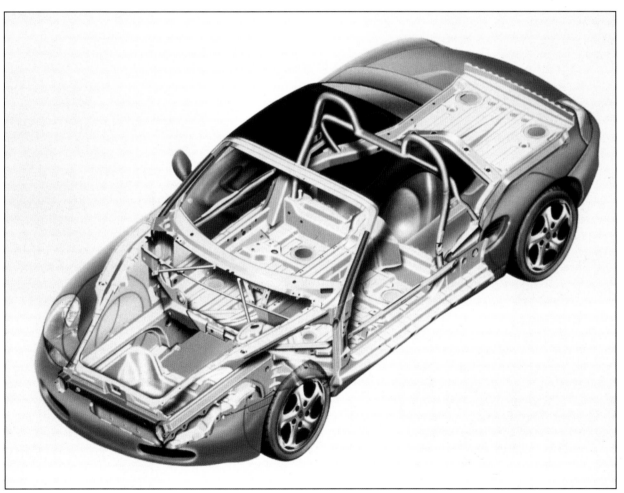

The front and rear inner structures of the Boxster are designed to collapse in a controlled manner in an accident to dissipate energy, directing it away from the passenger compartment. Further driver-passenger protection comes from high-strength steel roll bars behind them that work with the windshield frame to provide a safety cockpit. *Porsche AG*

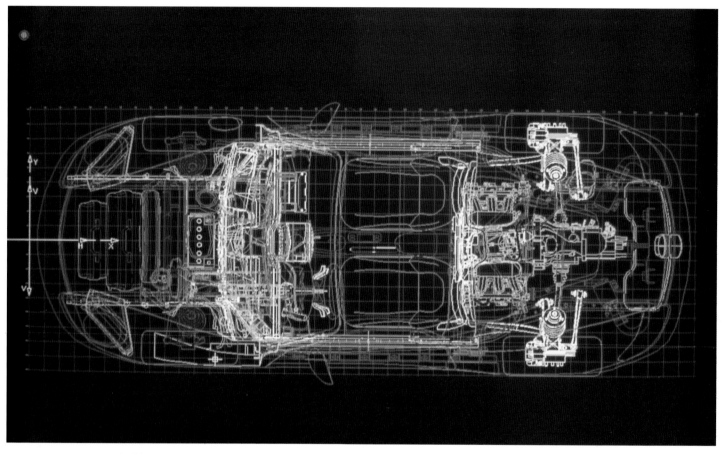

In this computer-generated graphic, it's easy to see the tight packaging of the Boxster, with the placement of the two-person cockpit, the midmounted drivetrain, and the suspension components. *Porsche AG*

and precise steering that make it easier to turn away from any dangerous situation you might encounter.

Passive safety is what you rely on when you're past the point of being able to save it at all and the accident is unavoidable. To save you in such disasters, Porsche engineers have used high-strength steel, which is carefully designed to route the energy that

must be managed in an accident away from the passenger compartment.

The front-end structure, which is patented by Porsche, has high-strength steel panels that are arranged in crush zones. This sounds rather gory, but is quite effective. Certain places in the car have been designed—in some cases through reinforcement—to deform in such a way that this bending eats up energy. Properly planned, these zones can control this deformation process and pass energy on from one to another, dissipating it while directing it away from the driver and passenger.

If the accident is that bad, the driver and passenger will also be protected by their shoulder harnesses and the airbag provided for each of them. If the duo in front includes a youngster in Porsche's optional child seat (properly installed), the airbag on that side will not go off as it has been electronically deactivated.

As of the 1998 model, Boxsters came with a little extra interior protection. Called POSIP, it adds side door panel-mounted airbags to the passive system. What sets these side bags apart from the usual is that they are rather large and designed to protect driver and passenger from hip to head level throughout the seat's fore-aft adjustments. What's more, their size and placement make them appropriate for the sports car whether the top is up or down.

There are other measures provided for protection, like the door's side impact panels and bulkhead reinforcement cross-members that are formed at high temperatures of a tough steel-boron alloy.

If a driver somehow manages to get a Boxster on its head, those inside the car are still protected. Behind them is a pair of special hard steel roll bars that are part of a structure that is bolted to the chassis and fits up and around the top of each seat. These padded bars work in conjunction with the windshield frame and can support 1.5 times the weight of the Boxster, turning the cockpit into something of a safety cubby hole.

Presumably, the average Boxster owner will never experience the inner workings of the car's passive system because

Stock tires for the Boxster are 205/55ZR-16s on the front and 225/50ZR-16s at the back. As an option, Porsche offers front 205/50ZR-17s and rear 255/40ZR-17s.

active system did the job, and the body and chassis play an equally important role in that.

The engineers had to consider another element of the body design during the design process: getting it built properly. So they spent hours deep in consultation with their colleagues from the production departments. Sounds boring, but this work was crucial to making the Boxster right and hitting that all-important $40,000 price promise.

Because there was a fundamental a part of the revolution at Porsche that was as crucial as the new management, simultaneous engineering and the lovable styling of the Boxster. Not only did the new sports car have to be ready on time, but it had to be built with the quality expected from Porsche in half the time needed to build the old 911.

Designing a top for the Boxster that would easily stow away despite the car's midengine design, which provides little space for the folded top, was a major engineering challenge. First plans called for a manual top to save weight and cost, but this idea was scrapped in favor of a one-motor power design

Right

Porsche engineers created a top-folding mechanism that maintains the top section over the driver and passenger as one piece, which is based on an award-winning part made of pressure-cast magnesium. As the top folds, it takes on the shape of a "Z" that folds down on itself, hence the name "Z movement."

Below

Folded and tucked away, the Boxster top disappears under a metal half-tonneau cover, producing not only a clean look but also excellent vision to the rear. Total time to put the top up or down? A mere 12 seconds.

CHAPTER SEVEN

PUTTING IT ALL TOGETHER

Craftsmen in blue bib overalls carefully fitting individual pieces to cars creeping along a slow-moving assembly line is the image many enthusiasts have of how Porsches are made. That's the way it used to be, with great stores of parts being drawn from by men who slowly hand-built each Porsche, like a series of one-off automobiles.

In reality, today's production line at Zuffenhausen may move more slowly than most, but you're more likely to come across a laser welding machine or an ecologically correct paint booth than a metal specialist tinkering to fit a body panel.

Don't bemoan this reality check. If Porsche still made automobiles in the so-called time-honored fashion, the Boxster might not even exist. If it did, most likely the price would be higher and the quality lower.

Modern automobile production processes have far outstripped both the quality and repeatability of the old methods. The world's best cars used to be painstakingly assembled by hand; the opposite seems to be true today.

The entire philosophy of automobile assembly has gone through an important transformation, not just at Porsche, but throughout the automaking business. While some of this change involves the actual devices—robots, computer-aided-manufacturing, etc.—that are used to assemble the automobiles physically, the real changes have been in thinking and processes.

It begins in the initial stages of a new car design. In the past, most automakers would design and develop an automobile first and then let their manufacturing experts figure out how to build it. These days, the production department is part of the design process from the beginning, advising what can and can't be accomplished simply in the assembly halls. Designing-in this "ease of assembly" is just another aspect of simultaneous engineering in which all the disciplines involved in creating and producing an automobile work together from day one.

Other important members of those simultaneous

Boxster body panels are delivered just in time by BMW to Porsche's Werk 3 building in Zuffenhausen, where they are welded into the car's bare unit body. *Porsche AG*

engineering teams are representatives of major parts suppliers. At some point along the design path, they will be chosen to be the exclusive supplier of one particular part or assembly. With that contract might come the responsibility to do the detail engineering of that part and its creation. This could be a simple piece, but it might also be a complex component, like the Boxster's seats, brake assemblies, the front axle, or the complete dashboard, which are delivered as finished subassemblies that are then bolted into the Boxster. Another responsibility passed on to these suppliers is a new attitude in which quality is paramount . . . no rejections, no excuses.

What's more, a modern automaker doesn't want a warehouse full of those parts, but to have them delivered

Using both robots and men wielding welding equipment, the Boxsters are assembled using a variety of techniques that were added to Werk 3 specifically to increase the quantity and quality of the cars built by Porsche. *Porsche AG*

just-in-time to be added to the automobile, whether the piece is something as small as a switch or as major as bare body panels and major subassemblies. Porsche is already cramped for room in its Zuffenhausen factory and doesn't need to devote space to large parts repositories. So companies that supply parts for Boxsters—complete dashboards, steering systems, brake assemblies, etc.—are given a 10-day notice of what parts will be needed when at the factory.

Three days before pieces are to be delivered, the suppliers get a detailed schedule of exactly what parts will be needed when and their sequence, like letting Recaro know the order of the colors and options needed in the seats they will be delivering. Unlike the old days, when warehouses were full of valuable parts that would be needed eventually, pieces are now delivered just-in-time to go from loading dock to assembly line and onto the car. No wasted time, no wasted space.

Adding new models to the assembly isn't something at which Porsche has a lot of practice. Before the Boxster, the company hadn't integrated a new model into the production line in the 18 years since the 928 arrived. Production techniques at Zuffenhausen hadn't been substantially altered in decades, and were as hidebound as the traditional system of skilled craftsmen who could create an automobile out of a storehouse of not-always-perfect parts. If this system had continued, Porsche could have lost its independence to another automaker, and ended up related to a company like Volkswagen in the same way Jaguar and Aston Martin are to Ford . . . as a subsidiary.

And then along came Wendelin Wiedeking, who knew full well that "pride goeth before the fall." Unafraid to fight tradition, the new board member of Porsche did the unthinkable, making changes at the top levels of management, slimming down the organization.

Next, he began taking company personnel, from those in charge of the assembly line to those who worked on it, to Japan to study that country's manufacturing techniques. This was no easy thing in a society that was convinced it already knew how things should be done. In a November

After being assembled in Werk 3, each Boxster body is transported to Werk 2 through an enclosed, glass-sided bridge high above Porschestrasse. After arriving in the second building, it goes to the paint shop.

1997 interview with Bill Sharfman of *Automobile* magazine, Wiedeking explained, "We went to Japan to benchmark the Japanese system, and not just to do a walkthrough. For three months we defined precisely what we wanted to learn, and we built teams. Then we went to Japan, went to the plants, watched precisely what was happening. At night we weren't sitting at the bar—we were in conference rooms. We always had two teams for each task, to make sure that we weren't missing anything."

Working on a very tight time schedule, Wiedeking then took the even bolder step of hiring Japanese consultants to help Porsche revamp its entire production system.

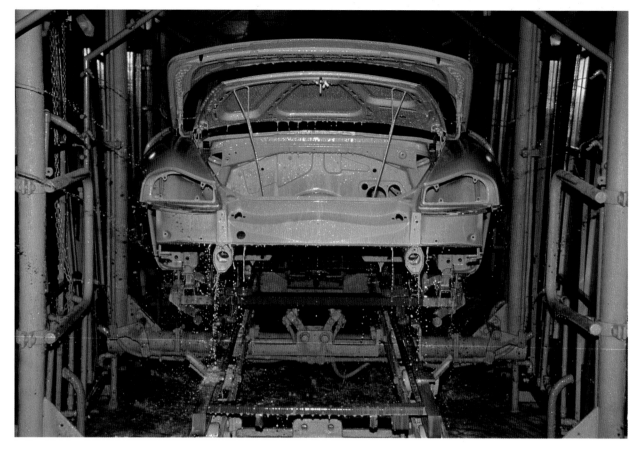

Before every Boxster body is painted, it goes through a variety of dips that both clean the body and add layers of protection against rust. *Porsche AG*

The result was a revolution in production thinking at Porsche that took it from being a traditional craft-based automaker rapidly pricing itself into the low-volume automotive stratosphere—up there with Ferrari—to an efficient assembler of automobiles that can profitably put the Boxster up against a pair of sports cars from two German giants, Mercedes-Benz' SLK and BMW's Z3. So dramatic was the conversion that it earned Porsche and Wiedeking a chapter in *Lean Thinking* by James P. Womack and Daniel T. Jones, a follow-up to their excellent book about

automobiles, *The Machine That Changed the World*. What Wiedeking was trying to accomplish—and apparently has—is nicely described in the subhead to *Lean Thinking*: "Banish Waste and Create Wealth in Your Corporation."

Not only do these modern methods save space and create better automobiles, but they dramatically cut the time it takes to build cars. The 933 (the old-generation 911) required around 100 hours to build. A Boxster or 996 (the new 911) needs about 50 hours to go from parts and preassembled modules on the loading dock to a finished automobile.

Asked how difficult it was to make the changes he brought about at Porsche, Wiedeking, who was educated as an engineer, states, "Nothing is easy in life. You must have a vision. You must be able to bring this vision over to your team and to make sure that things really happen."

While many executives can make comments like this, few have Wiedeking's ability to make them work, to which he comments, "I think the difference is that the chairman must understand that if you say something, you must be able to set the direction of the rest of your organization.

"If I walk through the factory, I know what I want to see. I notice if something is not going in the right direction. My experience is that I know what I'm talking about. It is absolutely necessary to have the experience and the knowledge to understand that when a strategy is defined what must happen if the strategy is to be adapted to reality.

"Most people are too far away from the day-to-day business, too far away from the reality. They can make a good drawing and they can print it, but to make it alive is the critical task. And this is only possible if you are able to

Boxsters are painted both by robot and by hand. These environmentally correct methods of painting are part of the 26-step protection system that allows Porsche to offer a 10-year warranty against rust-through. *Porsche AG*

In Werk 2, the Boxster's 2.5-liter flat-six are hand-assembled. At first it's difficult to tell the roadster's engine from the 911 flat-sixes, but differences in cylinder heads and intake systems later separate one from the other.

notice personally if there is a change going on. Not in the financial statements, but in the reality of the organization in your factory."

About the only thing more remarkable than what Wiedeking did at Porsche is his age. Born in 1953, he studied engineering in Aachen and earned a doctorate in 1983. After five years as an assistant to the Porsche board of management member who looked after production, he left for a company called Glyco Metallwerke and within two years was its chairman. So Wiedeking was only 38 when he returned to Porsche in 1991 to head production. Just a year later he was the board's spokesman, and the year after that named chairman. And all this is in a country in which executives used to spend decades earning their stripes.

Wiedeking's new reality at Porsche did not require new factories at Porsche manufacturing center in Zuffenhausen. Oldest of Porsche's buildings there is Werk 1, which was first occupied in 1933 and was all the company needed in its early years. These days the original factory serves as the company's headquarters and for customer service.

The main road in front of Werk 1 is appropriately called Porschestrasse and on its other side is Werk 2. Built in 1952 and taking up some of the space once occupied by the well-known body maker, Reutter, this is where Porsche engines are made and where the bodies are painted and put through final assembly.

Newest of Porsche's buildings, Werk 3, is on the same side of the street as Werk 1 and is the shop in which bodies are welded up from their basic pieces. And that's where a Boxster begins. Through doors in Werk 3 come the panels that will become Boxsters, received just in time from their supplier: BMW. That's right, the famous Bavarian automaker stamps the sheet metal for both new-generation Porsches, but given BMW's reputation for quality, who is to complain?

A combination of men and machines—some 70 robots—begin to assemble the many parts using a variety of methods for joining metal, five of which Porsche added when it upgraded the assembly line for the Boxster and new 911.

The most dramatic of the processes conjures of old images of James Bond about to be sliced in half by Goldfinger's laser. Except that the powerful robot laser welders at Porsche are used for joining the doors' structure and sheet metal by essentially melting seams of the two pieces together so they become one. Medium-frequency welding is utilized to fuse sheets of metal that have different thicknesses, a technique that aids in increasing the structural rigidity of the Boxsters.

The nine aluminum sheet-metal pieces that make up the lightweight aluminum hardtop are combined by 178 punched rivets, a system that doesn't require drilling holes for the steel rivets, which are punched right into the pieces of aluminum, joining them together.

Porsche uses a new clinching system for the front and rear deck lids that molds parts together under very high pressure to form one piece. Lastly, it uses what's called a whirl spray to apply a fine layer of adhesive to a number of top and door parts that are then glued to their appropriate other half and heated to 180 degrees Celsius to harden the "glue." Old-hand Porsche enthusiasts shouldn't be put off by this use of bonding rather than welding to assemble the Boxster, because not only does it do an excellent job of holding the metal together, but in the process it helps damp vibrations.

As the car skeleton works its way through the body shop, flying sparks of light confirm spots as they are welded and showers of sparks rush off grinding and smoothing

wheels. The Boxster begins to take shape. Soon it is quite a pretty bare metal hull, ready for the paint shop. The Boxster body enters a glass-walled bridge through which it is transported high above Porschestrasse, across to Werk 2 on the other side of the street.

Next comes a series of cleansing baths and antirust body treatments that, with Porsche's well-known hot-galvanized body panels, allow the automaker to give its cars a 10-year rust-through warranty. Then into the paint booths, which meet all the stringent German antipollution laws and involve water-based painting systems in which both robots and men apply the paint.

The Boxster's now colorful body shell is almost concealed by protective coverings for its trip along the assembly line. More and more parts of the car are bolted in place, many of them being the large subassemblies that

While Porsche assembles all its engines, the transmissions are received from outside suppliers: the five-speed manual from Volkswagen, and the Tiptronic automatic from ZF. After the engine is assembled, it is matched with its gearbox, and they are sent to the final assembly line.

were built up in a supplier's factory and delivered just in time as one module.

At about the time a Boxster body is being built in the shop and then painted, the pieces that will eventually become its 2.5-liter flat-six engine are being assembled across the road in Werk 2. Here's where the image of craftsmen carefully hand-building a Porsche still holds true. Shiny aluminum blocks are bolted to fixtures that allow them to be swiveled to ease the assembly process.

In a blur of power tools and torque wrenches, the engine is expertly assembled—crankshaft, rods, pistons, etc.—though at first it's difficult to tell the Boxster flat-six from the new 911's powerplant. As more pieces are added—cylinder heads, the intake manifold—the differences begin to show. When each engine is finished, it goes on a dynamometer for a 30-minute test. Powerplants are run-in for the first 12 minutes but then go through pre-programmed bursts to higher rpm as emissions, horsepower, and proper functioning are confirmed.

Any possible confusion over whether or not an engine is destined for a Boxster or 911 is over when the transmission is added and they are matched to their rear suspension.

The Boxster body has been welded together and painted. The engine has been assembled and mated with its transmission. The suspension parts have been received from their suppliers. All these pieces meet at what is called the marriage point.

Now the marriage takes place, a bellows on the bottom rig expanding so the engine, transmission, and suspensions are raised up into the body. Workers will bolt the units into place before the car slowly moves on to its next station.

Gearbox in front means a 911, gearbox behind is a Boxster. This rear drivetrain/suspension unit, plus the front suspension and steering are fixed to a rig that moves along a guided trail and has what appears to be a large bellows in its middle.

A marriage is about to take place. At least that's what Porsche calls this point on the assembly line where the drivetrain and suspension are added to the body. Riding along on overhead carriers are the Boxster and 911 bodies, which have been built up with still more important parts. This includes the cooling system. The radiators are so tightly and neatly fitted you can appreciate how difficult it was to package these elements.

As each high-mounted body reaches the marriage point, the rig with the engine and suspension swings in below it. The bellows expands, moving the drivetrain and suspension units up under the body where workers bolt them into place.

After the marriage of the body to its drivetrain and suspension, the Boxster is looking like something that will shortly be a finished automobile. It makes a 180-degree turn as the assembly line snakes back to the right and for what seems to be an inordinate amount of time, nothing happens. No parts are bolted on, no attention paid to this Boxster as it slowly moves along . . . or to the next Boxster or the 996 that follows them.

As the Boxster creeps along the Zuffenhausen assembly line, still more pieces are added, as here, where the rear bumper reinforcement bar is bolted in place. In the next step, the car's outer bumper cover will be installed.

Just as you begin to wonder why this valuable line space and time are wasted, an old 993 shows up in the sequence. When it gets to the seeming dead zone, you understand why that space is there . . . and why it takes twice as many hours to build the old car as the new ones. Instead of being ignored like the Boxster or 996, the 993 is descended upon by five workers. Going to both ends and sides of the older model, they beaver away the entire time the car is making the 180-degree arc, seemingly adding nothing but small, time-consuming parts.

At each work station, the Boxster takes on more of its final identity. On go bumper reinforcement bars, which are then covered by the outer plastic skin. The interior pieces are installed, as is the top, which is delivered as one finished component from Car Top Systems, the Porsche-Mercedes joint venture company that builds them and the folding metal hardtop for Mercedes SLK sports car, a major Boxster competitor.

Final drivetrain and suspension checks are made on a chassis dynamometer before the Boxster is taken for a drive. Through 12 to 15 miles of city, country, and autobahn driving, the spanking new Boxster is double-checked for everything from squeaks and rattles to making certain all the systems, from the gearbox to the heater, work properly. A slow run through a high-pressure water shower to check for leaks and the Boxster is ready to be sent to the distribution center and then to its new owner.

"Finnished" Boxsters

Despite everything Porsche did to make its Zuffenhausen factory capable of producing still more Boxsters, it wasn't enough. From the moment the world had a chance to understand just how good and affordable the Boxster is, potential buyers began hounding their local dealers for cars. Supply quickly lagged behind demand and Porsche distributors around the world faxed the factory asking for more Boxsters.

Porsche was hamstrung . . . and frustrated, a company that just a few years earlier was watching it sales dwindle now couldn't produce enough cars.

There was simply no way to increase production in the factory—which is limited to around 33,000 cars per year—and no way to increase its size. With the city of Stuttgart growing so quickly, land around the old factory had been bought up years ago. It would be difficult and expensive to expand.

Porsche couldn't even enlarge on its own land. The automaker had become such a legend that several old buildings on the site had been declared "industrial monuments" and couldn't be torn down or altered. A Porsche executive, commenting on one such building, told *Automotive News* reporter Lindsay Chappell, "We would've torn that building down 100 times by now if we could."

So if production was to be increased, it would have to be away from Zuffenhausen. BMW and Mercedes-Benz had built factories in the United States to meet increased demand. This was an obvious solution, but not Porsche's first choice. The company was concerned about the added fixed cost of such a facility. Like most automakers that needed added capacity at the time—including Mercedes

trying to decide where to build its M-Class sport utility— Porsche looked to eastern Europe, specifically to the Czech Republic. But that route was turned down. Volkswagen has long built cars in its Puebla, Mexico, factory and that country presented another choice, one that Porsche also rejected. There were numerous other possibilities, like the Pininfarina factory in which Ferraris and

Near the end of the final assembly line, the Boxsters get their folding convertible top. This modular unit is delivered ready-to-install from Car Top Systems, a joint Porsche-Mercedes venture that also makes the Mercedes SLK's folding metal hardtop.

When Porsche found it wasn't able to meet the world's needs for Boxsters, it had to find a second factory to build the sports cars. After considering such countries as Italy, America, and the Czech Republic, the company chose Valmet Automotive in Uusikaupunki, Finland, to build Boxster. *Joe Rusz*

Porsche production experts replicated their Zuffenhausen assembly system in the factory in Finland, ensuring that Boxsters built there would match the quality of those made in Germany. *Joe Rusz*

Cadillacs have been assembled. And, of course, further production in Germany was considered, possibly sharing a production facility with VW. That idea also faded after comparison to a rather unlikely location: Finland.

In a Baltic seaside town with the crazy spelling Uusikaupunki (roughly pronounced ooo-sue-COW-punke) is Valmet Automotive, a company with a 30-year history of building cars for European automakers. Best known of the products assembled there are Saab's 9-3 convertibles, but Valmet also put together Opel's Calibra coupe, which had gone out of production. The factory had available capacity, complete with a state-of-the-art paint shop.

For decades, the very idea of building Porsches outside Germany would have brought howls of complaint from the enthusiast motoring press and Porsche owners. Not anymore. It's appreciated these days that modern production systems put much more emphasis on process than people. A skilled, motivated work force is still a crucial part of quality production, but just as important are equally skilled suppliers, proper assembly equipment, and a vehicle that is designed to be built properly.

A Porsche production team went to work basically duplicating what the factory had in Zuffenhausen in Uusikaupunki. By May 1977, the first of the non-German

After completion, the Finnish Boxsters are loaded aboard a ship and taken to Porsche's German distribution center, where they are then sent to their final destination, many headed for the United States. *Joe Rusz*

Boxsters were on their pilot run through the Finnish factory. The following September 3, the Finns were ready to begin shipping customer Boxsters to Porsche's German distribution center.

Originally Porsche planned to have Valmet assemble 5,000 Boxsters each year, but within a few months of job one, the automaker had doubled its annual order.

Whether made in Germany or Finland, what makes a Boxster right was included long before the first car ever traveled down an assembly line. Knowing the new roadsters had to be right from the beginning, Porsche put its early prototypes through the assembly process, running them along Zuffenhausen's assembly line a year before series production began.

But ensuring the Boxster was right actually started back in early 1992, when Porsche's simultaneous engineering teams were thrashing over those first details and Wendelin Wiedeking's study groups were putting in their long days in Japan.

Waiting until those craftsmen in blue bib overalls were hand-building the cars in Zuffenhausen would have been too late.

CHAPTER EIGHT

DRIVING IMPRESSIONS

In 1949, the year Porsche first displayed its 356 coupe at the Geneva auto show, James Dean got his first car, a 1939 Chevrolet. You couldn't get two automotive events seemingly less connected, but just six years later, the names Porsche and James Dean would be forever linked.

As the 1950s progressed, the legends of both Porsche and James Dean grew. The automaker was making its name in competition events such as the 24 Hours of LeMans, the Mille Miglia, and the Carrera Panamericana. Dean was becoming well known as an actor on stage, television, and, finally, in movies. He received acclaim for *East of Eden* (released in April 1955) and then finished *Rebel without a Cause*, after which he finally had a chance to take a shot at racing. In March and May of 1955, Dean showed promise driving his first Porsche, a 1,500-cc Speedster, in races at Palm Springs, Bakersfield, and Santa Barbara. He bought a new Porsche 550 Spyder—one of the inspirations for the Boxster—but couldn't race it until after finishing filming of his third movie, *Giant.*

What Dean had bought was one of Porsche's production race cars, officially known as the Spyder Type 550/1500 RS. With a tube frame and hand-formed aluminum body, the open sports car weighed only 1,510 pounds. Power came from a version of the company's 1.5-liter flat-four fitted with dual overhead camshaft cylinder heads and rated at 110 horsepower at 6,200 rpm. With its successors, the RSK/RS60, the 550 Spyder was one of the inspirations for the Boxster.

On September 30, 1955, with *Giant* completed, Dean was rushing along rural California Highway 446 driving that new Porsche 550 Spyder, headed north to Salinas to race it for the first time. Another driver, having the unlikely name Donald Turnupseed, was heading the opposite direction in his 1950 Ford two-door coupe, about to turn left off 446 and onto Highway 41 to Tulare. For reasons still open to speculation today, the Ford driver

Having just finished the movie *Giant,* James Dean might have felt at home in the Central Valley as he passed these oil rigs on Highway 446 (now 46) on his way to Salinas, California.

turned left directly in front of Dean. The cars collided and Dean was killed.

The story is a legend in not just California, but also movie and Porsche history. Several times each year, groups make the pilgrimage from Los Angeles north to the spot where Dean died. Having never made that drive, and given the Boxster's tie to the type of Porsche Dean was driving, it seemed like an appropriate route on which to spend some time assessing the Boxster.

Like Dean and his mechanic, Rolf Wutherich, our trip began in Hollywood, going across the San Fernando Valley to the San Gabriel Mountains. Back then, you crossed the mountains on the old Grapevine highway. This was a somewhat treacherous three-lane road that connected southern and northern California. While famous Highway 101 is nearer the coast and quite picturesque, the Grapevine was the quick way north, whether to San Francisco or Sacramento, the state capital. Though you can still find portions of the three-lane road, it was replaced as a thoroughfare years ago by broad Interstate 5.

It was probably a bit hot the September day Dean made the drive, but for us it was one of those delightful days in early December when it begins cool and quickly warms. A day to enjoy the sunshine, and early on, I again found the main problem with the Boxster convertible top is that I forget how easy it is to use. That must sound odd to younger drivers, but for those of us who spent our formative sports car years driving MGs, Triumphs, and Austin-Healeys, the Boxster top is almost too good to be true.

For decades you didn't so much put up a sports car convertible top as erect it. This was no easy task and involved carefully unfolding the frame and fabric, getting

James Dean wound over the San Gabriel Mountains on the three-lane Grapevine highway to California's Central Valley. Although it was replaced by wide Interstate 5 year ago, portions of the Grapevine road are still used for local traffic.

your finger pinched in this or that, and trying to do up uncooperative snaps. Heaven wouldn't help if you were racing a fast-approaching thunderstorm, because you probably weren't going to get the top up in time. Even then, it was bound to leak.

Putting the top down wasn't much easier, and was only completed when you tried to stretch a tonneau that was made 7.5 percent too small over the folded top frame, which threatened to poke a hole in the tonneau.

So much for the good old days.

Lowering the Boxster top is a simple, five-part movement.

Stop. Leave the ignition on, and put on the hand-brake. Reach up and unlatch the locking lever. Swing the locking lever to the rear. Hold down the electric top's operating switch as the top folds. Whistle the first 12.5 seconds of your favorite tune. That's it. The top is down, nestled under a metal half-tonneau panel.

Want the top up? Reverse the previous instructions. It takes a total of 17 seconds, including raising the windows. I know, I timed it. I hope the engineer who designed the top received some sort of award for it. And my only concern is that at 20,000 miles the test car's plastic rear window was showing some small, permanent scratches, but Porsche tells us that the window is simple to replace.

Although the cross bows in the top are nicely finished, you can see some of the mechanism that raises the top, though it has a nice mechanical air about it. It is still just a fabric top, so you will hear road traffic through it and find yourself avoiding being right next to noisy 18-wheelers. Almost makes you wish they offered the option of a folding top with an interior headliner, like the new 911 Cabriolet.

Ultimately, however, it's the sealing that's important, and we couldn't find any windy drafts or whistling from our test car. We made a point of giving our test car a drive-through car wash to personally test it. Not a drop.

Those who live in seasonally nasty climates would want to take a close look at the Boxster's optional aluminum hardtop, which is easy to install and nicely finished inside. As with cars like Mercedes-Benz' 600SL, fitting the hardtop does more than just seal out the weather. Now the car isn't a roadster, but a close-coupled little coupe. The entire ambiance is different inside the hardtop Boxster as the road noise level plummets and you have a more secure feeling. It doesn't hurt one bit that the top is also nicely stylish, giving the car's upper a profile not unlike the closed Porsche 550 Spyders that raced at LeMans in 1955.

But take another 12 seconds and put the top back down, because that's how a Boxster should be driven if at all possible. With no top stack, vision to the rear is excellent and thanks to the see-through Lexan plastic wind blocker fixed in place between the roll hoops, you can cruise nicely at temperatures in the high 50s and still be quite comfortable.

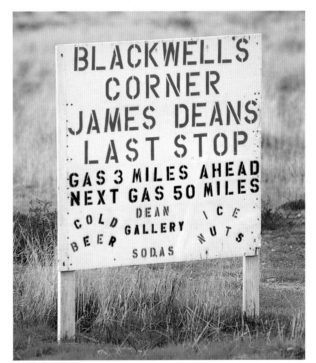

Retracing of Dean's last drive isn't complete without a stop at Blackwell's Corners, where he filled his gas tank and chatted with race drivers Bruce Kessler and Lance Reventlow before leaving for Salinas.

The stop at Blackwell's Corners features a small café and some James Dean memorabilia, including a copy of one of the traffic tickets the actor was issued the day he was killed.

Nestled securely in that little eye-in-the-storm created in the Boxster's interior, we settled into the drive up Interstate 5 and spent that freeway time looking around the Boxster's interior.

Porsche designers and engineers may have struggled with packaging everything inside the sports car, but it pays off. There's plenty of room for anyone up to about 6 foot, 1 inch to slide comfortably behind the wheel. The steering wheel has an in-out adjustment of about two inches. The leather-wrapped steering wheel provides a comfortable shape that works both for relaxed driving and for those who want a serious three-and-nine hand position for performance driving.

In another Porsche tradition, the ignition key is to the left of the steering wheel. Many years ago, drivers in the 24 Hours of LeMans had to run across the track at the start, jump into their car, start it, and race off. To make this easier, Porsche put the key on the left so the driver could use that hand for starting the engine, leaving his right hand free to work the shift lever.

Turn signals and high beam flasher are on an upper left-side steering column stalk. Boxsters with the optional on-board computer have a second, lower stalk on the left that can be moved to work you through several readouts on the bottom of the tachometer, from average fuel consumption to fuel tank range.

In the background, behind the Boxster, is the long straightaway James Dean was driving, heading into the late day sun, when Donald Turnupseed, who didn't see the little 550 Spyder, turned left at the intersection seen behind the Boxster. Dean couldn't avoid Turnupseed's big Ford coupe and in the collision the actor was killed and his passenger, Rolf Wutherich, badly injured.

One of the few irritations in the Boxster interior is the Becker radio, which has no knobs and too many tiny buttons to be used easily. To save on costs, Porsche had to buy an existing radio to use in the Boxster . . . but better versions than this one exist.

On the upper right-hand stalk are the windshield wiper/washer controls, while the one below it has the cruise control functions, which are a bit different than most cars, but easy to use and quickly learned.

Anyone who has driven an Audi A4 will recognize the air conditioning/heating controls. And that's just fine because the system works very nicely, with little need ever to take it off the "auto" setting. Fan volume is sufficient to quickly demist windows in damp climates and pump out an air conditioned breeze for fast cool-down times.

Just a few minor gripes about the interior:

Although they look rather elegant, the black switches are a bit too shiny, giving them something of an unfinished look.

It's too bad that in the long look at its past, Porsche wasn't able to include the radio. Many automakers have sensibly returned to easy-to-use knobs for tuning and volume. But using a preexisting radio design was part of the program to contain costs. Unfortunately, the Becker radio they chose for our Boxster has small, awkward buttons that require the driver to look away from the road and are not handy to use, an ergonomic fumble in an otherwise excellent interior.

The manual transmission shift lever, which changes gears by way of a cable, is rather positive, but does tend to hang up a bit in neutral when you're trying to get quickly from gear to gear.

Oh, and forget the cupholders, which have to be manually hung on the outboard vents and are a bit tenuous.

The Boxster's interior storage space consists of a series of cubby holes. There are two open receptacles at the bottom of the dash, a lockable area at the rear of the center console, and a bin in each door panel, half hidden under a flip-up armrest.

That armrest is nicely designed into the panel, giving the driver and passenger a handy pull for closing the door. It is also helpful for the passenger, who cannot only comfortably rest his/her forearm, but also get a grip when the driving becomes a bit spirited.

You get into the front and rear luggage compartments by way of a pair of driver's door sill-mounted levers that can't be opened when the door is shut. What's important about the front and rear spaces is that they are not only large (with the combined capacity of 11.2 square feet), but squared off and thus quite usable. The front area is notable for its deepness, while the rear is quite flat.

Also in the front "trunk" is the small inflatable spare tire, plus fluid reservoirs for the brake master cylinder and the windshield washer bottle. In the right-front corner of the rear luggage area is the sight level for the coolant expansion tank and the oil filler and dipstick.

There are two ways to check engine oil level in the sump. One is the traditional dipstick method, while the other is the equally traditional (for Porsche) instrument panel indicator, though now in digital form. When the engine is warm, you turn on the ignition switch and in the bottom of the right dial, temporarily displacing the digital clock, is an oil level gauge. It counts down through five seconds and then displays engine oil level for a few seconds before once again becoming a clock.

Here we were, thinking about digital readouts while tucked inside our wind-baffled interior while rushing down into California's Central Valley. At that point, James Dean and Rolf Wutherich were likely being buffeted around inside the spartan, noisy 550 Spyder . . . and probably loving it. At the base of the mountains, Interstate 5 cuts off to the left but, like Dean, we stayed straight on Highway 99, which aims north, with names like Bakersfield, Fresno, and Tulare on the road signs. At the town of Famoso, Dean turned off the main highway and to the west.

Once off the freeway, it isn't difficult to imagine what James Dean saw as he rushed westward along Highway

446. The Central Valley has been an agricultural center for some 100 years . . . and flat as a pool table for tens of thousands of years. Bright, hot, and blustery in summer, but damp, cold, and often enshrouded in fog in winter, the valley is highly productive but not particularly attractive. Roads tend to be dead straight, and with all that open expanse and little along the side to gauge your speed it isn't unusual to find the speedometer rising to 20 miles per hour above the posted limit.

As that momentum builds, even a small traffic impediment seems a bit irritating and it's a quick temptation to blow by the slow-moving pickup truck or farm tractor. The hazard is that it's also easy to be lulled into thinking how fast the other cars *aren't* traveling. This isn't an uncommon traffic phenomenon, says Porsche's design chief, Harm Lagaay, adding that they have the same problem in his native Holland, where it's call "plain blindness."

We stopped at Blackwell's Corner. Situated at the intersection of 46 and 33, this is "James Dean's Last Stop."

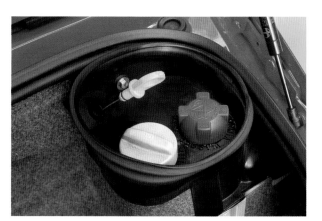

There are two ways to check the oil level of the Boxster flat-six. One is the standard method in which the driver reads the level on the car's dipstick, which is located in the right front of the rear luggage area and has a yellow handle. As in past Porsches, you can also note the level from inside the car. When you turn on the ignition switch, the digital clock in the bottom of the right-hand dial disappears and (if the engine is warm) five seconds later this oil level pictograph appears for a short time. Then it goes away and the clock reappears.

A small roadside sign even advertises that fact as you approach the combination gas station and eatery. Dean and Wutherich stopped at Blackwell's and chatted with famous race drivers Bruce Kessler and Lance Reventlow, who had also paused at this well-known wayside station.

It's easy to imagine Dean pulling onto the highway, the sun still high above the pretty low hills that separate the Central Valley from the Pacific Ocean coast, and burying the throttle of the 550 Spyder.

Coming out of the first set of hills is a straightaway that eventually ends in a long, gentle left-hand turn. Before the road bends, however, it intersects with State Route 41, which comes in from the right as you head west. Dean was on the stretch as Turnupseed approached him from the west, ready to turn left onto 41.

Stand at that intersection today and you can understand how the tragedy happened. Just before 6 P.M., the light was getting lower. The Porsche being so much smaller than the big sedans of the day, Turnupseed might have assumed it was farther away. Dean was going faster than another driver might expect. The cause of the accident is still questioned today, but the fact is it happened. When Turnupseed turned left in front of Dean, the small, light Porsche hit the big Ford coupe and was crushed. Turnupseed suffered minor injuries, Wutherich was severely injured, and James Dean was dead, one week before the opening of his second movie, *Rebel Without a Cause*.

Standing at that intersection in the fading light, it's just about impossible not to wonder what might have happened if Turnupseed hadn't turned left just then. If Dean had slowed. If . . . if . . . if . . .

You can continue on what is now 46 to Highway 101 south and use that four-lane road to get back to Los Angeles, or you take the little roads back. We chose the latter, which wound past vineyards and other agricultural crops. Nice as it is for cruising, this is the Boxster's forte. There's something rather sweet about the flat-six engine and the smooth way it sends the tachometer needle twisting to the right as you squirt down one lane and up another. Okay, the shifter is a little annoyance, but there's enough flexibility to the engine that you can keep gear changes to a minimum.

The steering is quick and sensitive, turning in easily right down to the very twisty bits. The car's basic handling attitude is understeer, but it's light and in the name of stability, not the heavy sort you experience in a sedan. Over-

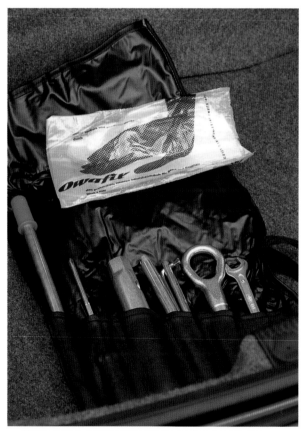

While some automakers skimp on the toolkits for their cars, Porsche still provides a rather complete set of tools, including not just specific implements for the Boxster but also the most necessary wrench.

One of the Boxster's ancestors is the first of Porsche's purposebuilt race cars, the 550 Spyder, seen here with a Boxster. This is the type of car James Dean bought to further his racing career, and it was while driving the 550 to a race that Dean was killed.

all, the ride and handling are a delightful balance, and I kept recalling Horst Marchart's words back in 1993 when he told us, "The car must be fun . . . a good sound. It should be a sporty car, but it can also be comfortable. It must not be harsh riding. . . ." Porsche seems to have gotten all that right.

We made our way back to 101 South, pointed toward Santa Barbara and then on to Los Angeles. Despite the coolness of the evening, we kept the top down for quite some time, and got to wondering how best to equip a Boxster.

Boxster designer Grant Larson commented that he liked the fact that owners are interested in making changes

to their Boxsters. It shows an interest in their new car. Knowing this would happen ahead of time, Porsche was all to happy to provide owners with a list of extras that runs out to 95 different choices.

There's even a special name for it: Tequipment. Many of the items are little dress-up pieces, like a steering wheel, gearshift knob, or handbrake lever with the look of carbon fiber, wood, aluminum, leather, or a combination. There are car covers, baby seats, sound systems, floor mats, a tailpipe extension, aluminum-color instruments, and even chrome-finished tire valves complete with the Porsche crest. There's an aero kit, though some of us would argue against the aesthetics of the rear lip spoiler.

As always, there's a debate over which wheel and tire combination looks best on the Boxster. Some of us side with the stock look and would only upgrade to the 17-inch wheels and tires. But there are also the alternative Dyno and Sport Classic designs, both in 17-inch diameter with Conti or Pirelli tires.

Those who like outdoor sports could opt for the Porsche roof transport system. Used with or without the hardtop, this is a unique frame that fits around and over the cockpit so you can affix skis, a surfboard, or other sports equipment. The ultimate payload? Porsche bicycles, which come in three flavors: $2,250, $4,500, or $6,000.

Perhaps the most significant add-on, however, is the aluminum hardtop. Weighing in at 55 pounds, the top has a proper electric rear window defroster for cold mornings and that coupe ambiance. At almost $2,300, it isn't an inexpensive option, but if, for instance, you had to make a long, hurried trip in a Boxster, even in fine weather, it might well be a more pleasant experience with the hardtop in place.

Powering the 550 Spyder was the same basic air-cooled flat-four used in other production Porsches then, but fitted with dual-overhead camshaft cylinder heads and two downdraft Solex carburetors, sized at 1,498 cc and rated at 110 horsepower.

Headed back toward Los Angeles in the dark, relaxed in the Boxster, I got to thinking about how it fits into the American scene. And about the enthusiasm Frederick Schwab, who heads Porsche in the United States, expresses for the car. He explains, "Half of the 911s we've sold in this country have been convertibles. We sell about 75 percent of Porsche's worldwide convertible production, and it's always been like that."

Then he adds, "The Boxster is a car for America. It has had a waiting list since before we told the public what it would really look like and what it would cost. We had people all over the country putting down deposits on a car when they didn't know what it would look like or what it could cost.

"To this day people ask me what is the ultimate demand for the Boxster and I tell them I don't know."

One suspects it will be several years before we find out.

This is the spartan interior of the sort of Porsche 550 Spyder James Dean was driving when killed. Dean's car didn't have the seat/shoulder belts seen in this Porsche museum-owned car, but they probably would have been of little help in the crash of his lightweight race car against the big Ford coupe.

CHAPTER NINE

THE REVIEWS ARE IN

No sooner had the cover been whipped of the Boxster show car at the 1993 Detroit Auto Show than it began to capture awards. Before the week was out, *Autoweek* had declared the Porsche concept car the "best of show." At the same time, the Boxster captured the hearts of not just the public but the journalists who wrote about it. We were also interested in seeing Porsche pull itself out of the soup, though the company's performance of the past few years had left us concerned.

With an open mind, however, journalists sat tight for the 42 months it would take to bring the Boxster to production. That unusually short for Porsche development time should have been our first clue that things had changed in Zuffenhausen. As rumors of the new sports car leaked into the magazines, often accompanied by a blurry photo of a black mysterious Boxster test car, we had trouble believing all we heard, particularly the continuing insistence on a promised price of $40,000. We kept wondering if something was getting lost in the conversion of Deutschmarks to dollars. Midengine? Flat-six? Disappearing electric top? $40,000? Sounds too good to be true.

Thos L. Bryant (the editor of *Road & Track*) and I were able to confirm all but the price part of the Boxster formula on a warm summer's day in July 1996. Out of the door of Porsche's traditional headquarters in Zuffenhausen rolled a spanking new silver Boxster. Despite decades of attending the rollouts of new cars, it's rare that you view one you know is going into the history books. The Mercedes-Benz 6.3-liter V-8 sedan, the original Honda Accord, the unveiling of the F40 in the presence of Enzo Ferrari . . . and the day Porsche stepped out of the soup with the Boxster.

We spent the day falling in love with the new Porsche, rushing along the roads that lead from village to forest and back in the area around Weissach. We took our time just looking at the Boxster, with its wonderfully balanced design that pays respects to Porsches of the past without imitating them.

Porsche's Boxster is slightly bigger than its competition, measuring 169.9 inches long and 70.0 inches wide versus the BMW's 158.5 inch/68.5 inch and the Mercedes' 157.3 inch/67.5 inch. At 50.8 inches high, the Boxster is identical to the Mercedes and only 0.1 inch taller than the BMW.

BMW's entry in the small sports car market is the American-made Z3. While it is available with a four-cylinder engine, the company's real competition for the Porsche is the version with a 189-horsepower, 2.8-liter straight-six. The car features independent suspension at both ends and has a base price of around $36,000.

The Boxster had gotten somewhat larger on its way to the assembly line. We noted in *R&T*, "To convert the show Boxster to production it grew a bit, mainly to meet safety regulations. With safety bumpers and door protection beams came more size, the production Boxster's overall length at 171.0 inches, up from the show car's 162.0. Wheelbase increases from 94.5 inches to 95.2, width from 68.5 to 70.1, and height from 48.8 to 50.8 inches." When

Mercedes-Benz takes on the Boxster with its German-built 230 SLK, which is unique because of its metal hardtop, which folds neatly into the rear luggage compartment. Power for the Mercedes is from a 185-horsepower, 2.3-liter supercharged four. Cost of the SLK is about the same as the Boxster.

we had a chance to see a Boxster in traffic it did appear larger than we expected. That size, however, also means a spacious cockpit for two guys the size of Tom and me, plus luggage space to hold all the camera equipment a person could need in one day.

Peter Robinson, a lanky and likable Aussie-resident-in-Italy, is one of the most-published automotive journalists in the world. "Robbo" did the first-drive story for *Car and Driver*. In an article in November 1996 subtitled, "The winner, by a knockout," he began by writing, "If there has been a contest going on among BMW, Mer-

cedes-Benz, and Porsche to see which German automaker could build the best-performing small roadster, Porsche should be passing out cigars right now. The new mid-engined Boxster is all Porsche, a simply marvelous sports car and the most dynamic and exciting of all the new generation of two seaters.

"Where the BMW Z3 is soft and affordable and the Mercedes SLK so civilized it's hedonistic, the Boxster is pure, taut, and sparkling with desirability."

As soon as the Boxster was released, automobile magazines began hounding Porsche for cars they could put

through their road test procedures. *Road & Track*'s Joe Rusz went to Germany to do its first test. An admitted Porschephile who owns a like-new early 911, Rusz began his trials with a high-speed run down one of Germany's Autobahns. Driving ahead of another Boxster, he watched it in his rearview mirror, also noted its size, but then pointed out that it is "314 pounds lighter than the 911 (the older 993 version). And structurally, 20 to 30 percent stiffer, despite being a roadster. Trundling along the Autobahn, the Boxster's rigidity was evident. The car felt impressively solid. And proved to be astonishingly quiet at near-century-mark speeds, as I discovered when we finally reached the Wurzberg-Stuttgart Autobahn, last leg of our journey."

Calling the flat-six engine "incredibly smooth and quiet," Rusz helped put the Boxster through the magazine's road test procedure, pulling down a 6.1-second 0–60 mile per hour time in the process. About the only complaint he had is one echoed by many who drive the Boxster when he wrote he'd pay extra "for a proper shift linkage rather than the cable shifter I sparred with, mostly on four-three downshifts."

Major auto magazines were also looking forward to comparing the Boxster directly to its obvious rivals, BMW's Z3 with the 2.8-liter six and Mercedes-Benz' supercharged 230 SLK. *Car and Driver* did just that in April 1997 and declared the Boxster the winner. Writing the road test was Pat Bedard, possibly the best engineer-writer in the business.

Of the engine he wrote, ". . . it's a sweet contributor to this car's success. It makes whirring sounds, quite loud and clatter-free in a way foreign to Porsches. These whirs fade to the background when you're driving." He called the cockpit,

At the 1997 Frankfurt Auto Show, Porsche showed several Boxsters featuring optional factory equipment. One has a set of headrests (left) while the other car features an add-on (and not very attractive) rear lip spoiler.

". . . serene. Unless the top is down. Then, if the road is right, you hear organ-pipe resonances more beautiful than any since Bach when the intake and exhaust passages pass through their 5,200-to-5,500-rpm frequencies . . ."

As for the car's handling abilities, Bedard said, "The Boxster's cornering behavior is first-rate. The steering stays lively and responsive at the limit, and the rear tracks reliably behind. Porsche brags of a new way of managing deflection steer in the rear wheels. It works. This is not a tail-happy handler, never mind the reputation of mid-engine cars." And that from a man whose talent behind the wheel earned him drives in both the 24 Hours of LeMans and the Indianapolis 500.

In its comparison of the German trio of sports cars, *Road & Track* didn't rate the three so much as separate them, the BMW to the traditionalists, the Mercedes to "the enthusiast who places ingenuity and comfort slightly ahead of all-out sportiness," while the Boxster was recommended to the sports car purists.

Joe Rusz was again the author and this time had a Porsche with the Tiptronic 5-speed automatic gearbox. He didn't particularly like it. "Although the Tiptronic may be satisfactory for commuting in stop-and-go traffic, it's not really sporty . . . Zooming up and back along an Arizona two-lane, I found myself getting bored and thinking how out of character this gearbox is in an automobile that practically screams, 'Sports Car.' "

He still loved the car, however, asking, "Why buy a Boxster when the Bimmer is cheaper and the Benz (dare I say?) is more chic? Because it's a purebred, not a mongrel, but that's Porschespeak. The point is, you don't have to bow toward Zuffenhausen or light votive candles in memory of Ferdinand Porsche to appreciate the Boxster's distinctive shape, stylish and roomy interior, rich appointments, capacious front and rear luggage compartments and, most important, a top that stows away neatly behind a pair of Spyder-inspired roll hoops to unveil (ta da!) classic roadster lines—the 550's, the RSK's, the RS-60's. Spiced up with contemporary touches that reveal themselves the longer and harder you look."

Those glowing words from the automobile magazines echo the feelings of most people who drive the Boxster. William Jeanes, a well-known motoring journalist and editor of *Classic Automobile Register*, was so taken by the new Porsche, he bought one.

Granted, the Boxster has to prove itself over the years. It will evolve with more horsepower in a version called the Boxster S, and we will know more about the longevity of its many new systems. So there are still more chapters to be written about Porsche's Boxster, but the message so far is very promising.

As was the end of the Porsche's first year in America, when it won two more awards. *Car and Driver* magazine's January 1998 issue named the Porsche to its 10 Best Cars of 1998 list. Editor-in-chief Csaba Csere wrote, "Couple the Boxster's performance with the pleasure of a convertible top, which is particularly rapid acting and easy to use, as well as the practicality of front and rear trunks, the exhilaration of race-bred handling, and the glorious beauty of its show-car-inspired lines, and you have one of the most desirable cars of the year."

And just a half decade after the Boxster concept car was debuted at the Detroit auto show, *Automobile Magazine* took the occasion of the 1998 show to award the production Boxster its 1998 Automobile of the Year award.

Not a bad beginning.

SPECIFICATIONS

General Dimensions

Length	171.0 in/4315 mm
Width	70.1 in/1780 mm
Height	50.8 in/1290 mm
Wheelbase	95.2 in/2415 mm
Track, front/rear	
16-in wheels	57.7 in/1465 mm
	60.2 in/1524 mm
17-in wheels	57.3 in/1455 mm
	59.4 in/1508 mm
Ground Clearance	4.5 in
Luggage Capacity	5.2 + 6.0 cu ft
Fuel Tank Capacity	15.1 gal
Curb Weight	2,756 lbs
Weight Distribution front/rear	47/53

Chassis and Body

Layout	Midengine with rear drive
Body	Unit all-steel body with body panels hot-galvanized on both sides
Safety Equipment	Shoulder/lap belts, dashboard and door-mounted airbags for driver and passenger
Drag Coefficient	0.31
Suspension	
Front	MacPherson struts, lower A-arms, coil springs, tube shocks, antiroll bar
Rear	MacPherson struts, lower lateral links, toe links, coil springs, tube shocks, antiroll bar

Chassis and Body continued

Steering

Rack & pinion with variable power assist

Overall ratio 16.9:1

Turns, lock to lock..3.0

Turning circle ....35.8 ft

Brakes

Hydromechanical twin-circuit brake system, brake circuits acting individually on front and rear axles, Bosch ABS

Front....................................11.7-in. vented discs

Rear ....11.5-in. vented discs

Total swept area................................484 sq. in.

Wheels and Tires

Cast alloy with Pirelli or Conti radials

Standard

Front..........................6.0Jx16 with 205/55 ZR-16 tires

Rear ....7.0Jx16 with 225/50 ZR-16 tires

Optional

Front..........................7.0Jx17 with 205/50 ZR-17 tires

Rear ....8.5Jx17 with 255/40 ZR-17 tires

Powertrain

Engine

Six-cylinder, water-cooled boxer engine with aluminum crankcase and cylinder heads, dual overhead camshafts, four valves per cylinder, dry-sump lubrication

Bore . . . . .85.5 mm (3.37 in)

Stroke . . . . .72.0 mm (2.83 in)

Displacement . . . . .2480 cc/151 ci

Compression ratio 11.0:1

Engine output . . . . .201 bhp at 6,000 rpm

Max torque . . . . .181 lb.-ft. at 4,500 rpm

Maximum engine speed . . . .6,700 rpm

Fuel injection . . . . .electronic sequential port

Fuel grade . . . . .premium, unleaded

Transmission

5-speed manual or Tiptronic automatic

Transmission Ratios

	Five-speed manual gearbox	Five-speed Tiptronic S
1st gear	3.500	3.670
2nd gear	2.120	2.000
3rd gear	1.430	1.410
4th gear	1.030	1.000
5th gear	0.790	0.740
Final drive ratio	3.889	4.205

Clutch diameter . . . . . .240 mm (9.45 in.)

Performance (Source: *Road & Track*, December 1996)

Acceleration

0–30 mph . . . . .2.0 sec

0–40 mph . . . . .3.3 sec

0–50 mph . . . . .4.6 sec

0–60 mph . . . . .6.1 sec

0–70 mph . . . . .8.2 sec

0–80 mph . . . . .10.2 sec

0–90 mph . . . . .12.8 sec

0–100 ft . . . . .2.9 sec

0–500 ft . . . . .7.9 sec

0–1,320 (1/4 mile) . . . . .14.7 sec @ 93.2 mph

Braking

From 60 mph . . . . .120 ft

From 80 mph . . . . .210 ft

Control . . . . .excellent

Brake feel . . . . .excellent

Overall brake rating . . . . .excellent

EPA Fuel Mileage

City . . . . .19 mpg

Highway . . . . .27 mpg

INDEX